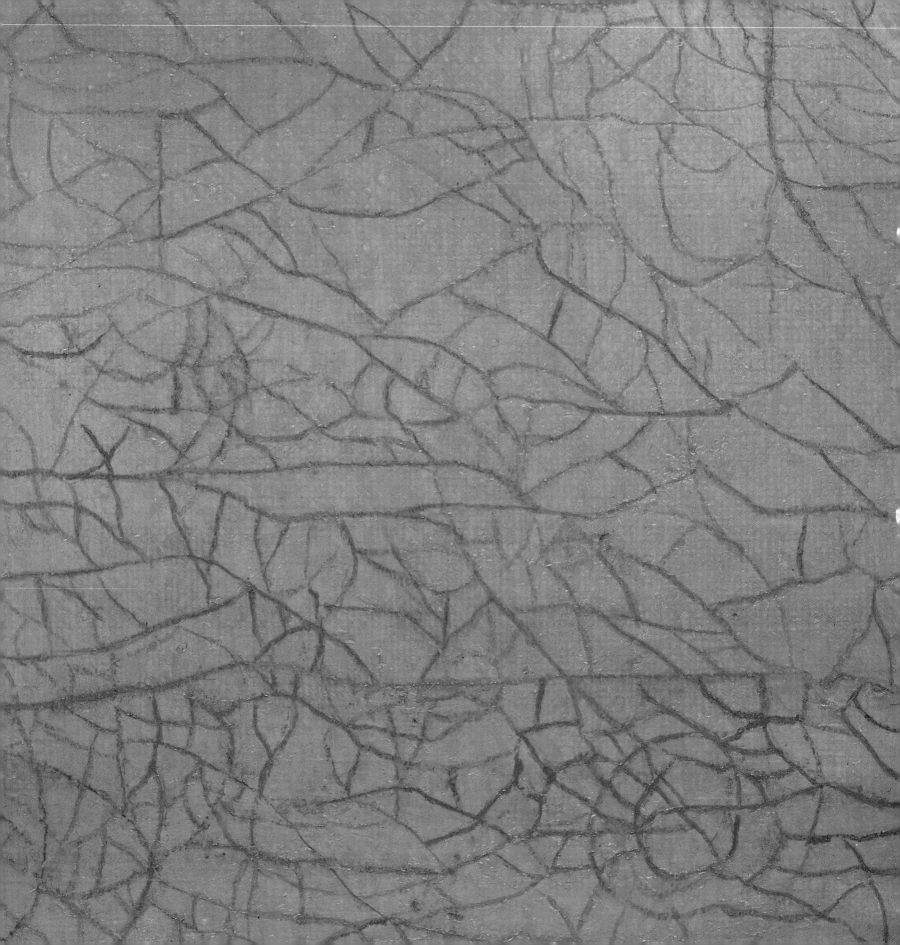

# SPANISH STYLE

# Spanish Style

## SUZANNE SLESIN, STAFFORD CLIFF & DANIEL ROZENSZTROCH

PHOTOGRAPHS BY

## GILLES DE CHABANEIX

FOREWORD BY
### PALOMA PICASSO

A GLIMPSE OF SPAIN BY
### MANUEL CANOVAS

DESIGN BY STAFFORD CLIFF
ART ASSOCIATE: IAN HAMMOND

CLARKSON POTTER
PUBLISHERS
NEW YORK

# ACKNOWLEDGMENTS

To Philip Cutler, whose love and enthusiasm for Spain, and all things Spanish, set us on the route to Spanish Style.

Published by Clarkson N. Potter, Inc., distributed by Crown Publishers, Inc., 201 East 50th Street, New York, NY, 10022. Member of the Crown Publishing Group.

CLARKSON N. POTTER, POTTER, and colophon are trademarks of Clarkson N. Potter, Inc.

Manufactured in Japan

Library of Congress Cataloging-in-Publication Data
Slesin, Suzanne.
    Spanish style/Suzanne Slesin, Stafford Cliff, Daniel Rozensztroch; photographs by Gilles de Chabaneix.        p.        cm.
    1. Spain – Social life and customs. 2. Architecture – Spain – History. 3. Interior decoration – Spain – History – 20th century.
I. Cliff, Stafford. II. Rozensztroch, Daniel. III. Title. DP48.S57 1990
946 – dc20        90-37641 CIP

ISBN 0-517-57438-1
10 9 8 7 6 5 4 3 2 1
First Edition

CREDITS:
Page ii
Detail from *The Young Virgin Praying*, 1632-3 by Juan de Zurbaran: The Metropolitan Museum of Art, Fletcher Fund, 1927 (27.137), Copyright © 1985 Metropolitan Museum of Art. (27.137)
Page iv-v
*Still Life with Sweets*, 1622 by Juan Van der Hamen: The Cleveland Museum of Art, John L. Severance Fund. (80.6)

IN SPAIN: Special thanks to Santiago Cortes in Madrid; Fernando Amat, Brigitte Szenczi, Juan Antonia Manas, and Vicenç Ferrán in Barcelona; José Luis Gil de la Calleja and Aurora Poveda Amadon in Minorca.
Thank you also to all who let us photograph their homes, and those who made suggestions, and helped all along the way: Lluisa Albacar i Gelabert and Betina Pons of the Patronat Municipal de Turisme de Barcelona, Manuel Anvarbe, Manel Armengol, Fernando Benjumeca, Carmen Bozano, Fernando and Fina de Calderon, Elena Calderon, Juli Capella, Xavier Carulla and Luise Segarra, Rafael Cidoncha, Cristian Cirici and Anna Bricall, Pepe Cobo, Victoria Combalia Dexeus, Pascale Dufournier, Patrick and Queen Dupin, Bibi Escalas, Antonio Fernandez, Juan Francisco, Ramon Gari de Sentmenat, Rosina Gomez Baeza, José Buil Mayral, Eugenio F. Granell and Amparo Segarro Vicente, Maria Joan, Clementina Liscano, Jose Ramon Lizarazu Esnaola, Carmen Llopis Hernando, Carmele Marchante, Concha Marques, Raphael and Mar Ann Marsans, Javier Martinez Senosiain and Rosa Maria Casas, Juan Antonio Martinez, Miguel Mila, Miralda, Jose Juanpere Miret and Luisa Casachs Nubiola, Antonio Moragas, Ignacio Muñoz, Paco Muñoz and Sabine Deroulede, Javier de Olaso, Rafael Ortiz, Marga Paz, Lluis Porqueras Domenech, Blai Puig Gausachs, Dolores Puig i Rui, Tom Puig, Gabriel Ordeig Cole, Maria Pena Raso, Stella Pincas, Carlos Riart, Enrique Ribero, Violette Roda Gil, Rosario Rodriguez Aguado, Salvador Sanchez Barbudo and Carmen Cobo, Mercedes de Sentmenat Fabregas, Miquel Servera Blanes, Pep Sunol, Joan Mari Tur, Oscar Tusquets, Joana Vivel, and Jose Viader.

IN PARIS: Catherine, Martin, and Simon de Chabaneix, Laurence Dumaine, Mariette Landon, Jean-François and Helene Maury, Bettina Mortemard, Veronique Pataud, Andrée Putman, Marguerite and Isabelle Rispal, and Elisabeth Vedrenne.

IN LONDON: Maurice White of Front Page Graphics, Tony Tortoroli and Bill Fentress of Campaign Colour, the Textile Department at the Victoria and Albert Museum, Robin Mason for the Catálogo illustrations, Jonathon Adams for the half-title and title page paintings, Ian Hammond for production, Jonathan Scott, and Mr. Hormozi, Ali Hormozi, and Chris Ricketts at Momento Print Ltd.

IN NEW YORK: Michael Adams, Judyth van Amringe, Jorge and Marentza Castillo, Daniel Aubry and Clodagh, Xavier Corberó, Roberta Cores and Evelyn Mariperisena of the Spanish Tourist Office, Jill Faust, Emily Gwathmey, Karen Kligerman, Gina Iaderosa, Inmaculada de Habsburgo, Rosi and Pierre Levai, John Loring, John Margolies, Bill Nave, Brian Nissen and Montserrat Peccanins de Nissen, Jeffrey Osborne, Virginia Pepper, Sofia Parenas, Elsa Peretti, Monique Silverman, Paul Siskin and Perucho Valls, Michael, Jake, and Lucie Steinberg, Daniel Tilkin, and Barbara Toll and Marlene Wetherill.

Thank you especially to Paloma Picasso for her foreword and to Manuel Canovas for his glimpse of Spain. Thanks also to David Diamond, Raquel Gershberg and Beth Dunlap for the Catálogo; to our editors Lauren Shakely and Roy Finamore of Clarkson N. Potter; our publisher Carol Southern and our agents, Lucy Kroll and Barbara Hogenson.

March 1990

SUZANNE SLESIN, NEW YORK
STAFFORD CLIFF, LONDON
DANIEL ROZENSZTROCH, PARIS
GILLES DE CHABANEIX, PARIS

# CONTENTS

FOREWORD ix

A GLIMPSE OF SPAIN 1

1. IMAGES OF SPAIN 4

2. LIVING IN SPAIN 16

3. ELEMENTS OF SPANISH STYLE 28

4. SPANISH ACCENTS 50

5. THE PALACE 100

6. FAMILY TRADITIONS 136

7. MODERN VIEWS 186

8. ON VACATION 228

CATALOGO 289

INDEX 298

# *FOREWORD*

## BY PALOMA PICASSO

It took me many years to understand what it

What's wonderful about Spain has always been the *idea* of Spain. There is

meant to be part Spanish. I grew up speaking

something mythical, something grander than life, that Spain has managed

French, and my father never spoke Spanish

to retain, even though it's a real country with people living in it every day.

to me. I didn't go to Spain until I was 18.

Spain deals in life and death all the time. It's all or nothing. Very extreme.

So for many years I thought Spain was just

Spain is the smell of heat. During the day the heat is so strong it almost

bullfights and flamenco. And Ava Gardner.

obliterates every other smell. But when the sun comes down, the smell of

As a child I always looked to her as a model

jasmine, all those kinds of flowers, starts to flourish. Every night all of

of what a woman should be. It's funny.

Spain is washed. Around three or four in the morning, city employees

Ava Gardner was not Spanish, and yet she

clean each city with water. Five minutes later, the streets are completely

personified Spain for me. Actually, she

dry. There has been such heat on those paved stones all day long that it

found it for herself too. Sometimes you

just drinks up all the water in seconds. That also helps bring out the

recognize things in yourself when you visit

smells. The idea of cleaning, of caring for cities, is very important and, I

a certain place. She must have felt that.

think, unique to Spain. Spain is more about the *people* than anything else.

It is this idea of being well put together. Very often, around seven o'clock,

you see the parents go out with their children. Boys are in white shirts that

have been perfectly ironed, girls are in crisply starched dresses, and they still have their hair wet because they've just had a bath before.

When I think of Spain I think of a certain harshness in the scenery. Brown hills. Gnarled olive trees. The people are generous. Nature is not. That's what makes the spirit of the country.

I went back to Andalusia two summers ago, and I realized then how typically Andalusian my father was. The way of the Spanish seems more human – not intellectual but natural. Everybody is on the same level. I remember my father would always speak to people as though he'd known them all his life. Whenever we would be having lunch somewhere, you could see that people were excited to be sitting next to Pablo Picasso. Sometimes they would come up to us and talk. When we left, my father would always say, "These are our childhood friends." That was the kind of relationship he would establish with people, which is very generous in a way because there are no barriers.

What is Spanish? I think it is a mixture of all these things. A certain civility. Something rigorous. A rigor mixed with a very grand gesture. It's what you see in the flamenco dress, and in the flamenco dance. Something that comes really from inside, and the gesture is glamorous and open and generous.

*Paloma Picasso is a New York – based designer of accessories (for Lopez-Cambil Ltd.) and jewelry (for Tiffany & Co.).*

**PRECEDING PAGE**   Still Life with Silver Gilt Salvers, *1624 by Juan Bautista de Espinosa © Christie's.*

**LEFT**   Soller *by Santiago Rusinyol © Museo de la Abadia de Montserrat. Index photo.*

**RIGHT**   Montroig, el Poble i englesia, *1919 by Joan Miró © ADAGP, Paris and DACS, London 1990.*

# A GLIMPSE OF SPAIN

## BY MANUEL CANOVAS

My father's family descended from the "old Christians" who played an active role in the reconquest of the kingdom of Murcia from the Moors. Like all the *hidalguia* of southern Spain, my father's family preferred arms to the arts. My father, however, preferred art. As the youngest son he was free to choose, so in 1920 he came to Paris, a city he adored. Thus I was born in Paris in 1935 into a family that cultivated art in all its forms. It was decided that I would be an artist – not a common choice in those days. From a very young age I was introduced to – and sometimes had imposed on me – drawing lessons, the Florentine Renaissance, perspective, anatomy, 18th-century France. But I was never taught the magic of color; fortunately, this was a natural gift.

To understand Spain it is important to remember that at least seven peoples, seven very different and conflicting cultures were mixed into one incredible medley creating the origin of the Spanish kingdoms: Iberians, Celts, Phoenicians, Carthaginians, Romans, Visigoths, and Moors. To complete the intricate mosaic there were three religions – Christianity, Islam, and Judaism. This was the seething pot that the "Catholic Kings," Ferdinand and Isabella set out to unify into the one nation of Spain.

Spain is a universe of light and darkness, a world of black and white. Spain is arrogant through the pride of its poor; however, it is rich in its mystical soul. It is a land of contradiction. Like the enormous coats of arms sculpted on the sober facades of the old Castillian houses. There is little color but great depth. All is simultaneously frozen and melting. The landscapes, the people, the customs – they are not "sweet." They are noble.

Sometimes, in old Castille, a village and its castle blend together into the color of the surroundings; they are built of the same earth, of the very same dust. In Estramadura, an abandoned fortress stands out, navigating alone through an ocean of desert. Stark architecture. Pure lines. Austerity becomes pride, never vanity.

In the end, nothing is less agreeable to a Spaniard than to be agreeable; nothing pleases less than to please. Spaniards have only a vague notion of time – a taste for the approximate that was probably unconsciously inherited from the Moors – and they are fairly thin-skinned. However, they are unequalled in their generosity and capacity for the elegant gesture. They will fight over who holds the door or who pays the check. Nothing is worse for a Spaniard than to be "small" or "stingy." A Spaniard's friendship may be fussy, but it is truly faithful.

*Manual Canovas, S.A. was founded in 1963. This international company designs and distributes luxury products for all aspects of the home: textiles, linens, tableware, beachwear, and home fragrances.*

**PRECEDING PAGE** *"Fiesta en la Venta" by José García Ramos from* Diccionario enciclopedico ilustrado de flamenco, *Madrid. CinterCo.*

**RIGHT** *A romantic tower in ruins sits on top of the craggy hillside that dominates Zahara de la Sierra, one of the white villages of Andalusia.*

# CHAPTER 1

# IMAGES OF SPAIN

Corrida, feria, flamenco — in these three words are distilled the essence of Spain and its time-honored customs.

The colorful spectacle of the corrida, or bullfight; the feria, a festival that takes place during Holy Week and includes long processions, the most fervent of which are held in Seville; and the flamenco, a tradition of dance and songs, the whole an artistic performance that mirrors the Andalusian soul — these are more than folklore. They maintain, even today, strong links to the Spanish identity that was forged long ago.

**ABOVE**  *A window in Cáceres in Estremadura is protected by an iron grille and surrounded by a sgraffito border of dolphins.*

**RIGHT**  *A farmer leads his cows home over the cultivated slopes outside the town of Córdoba, in Andalusia.*

**TOP**  The symbolic image of the castle in Spain is brought to life by the Alcazar, a romantic 14th-century castle perched above Segovia, an old Castilian town.

**ABOVE**  The road to the white villages of Andalusia offers dramatic views of the numerous rural dwellings that have been carved into the rock and that are often lived in by gypsies.

**RIGHT**  Houses with time-worn plaster facades line a narrow street in Seville.

There are few stronger images that bring to mind the passion and romance of Spain than the Spanish woman. She is Carmen, Bizet's flamboyant heroine; she is the Lady of Spain of pop music fame. And whether a gypsy flamenco dancer or of aristocratic lineage, she is sensual — with a strong legacy of the Orient — and idealized.

**LEFT AND RIGHT**   *The Spanish woman has been interpreted in multiple guises that reflect her many roles in sculpture and painting, as well as in daily life.*

The *corrida de toros,* or bullfight, in which man challenges the bull, first appeared in Spain in the 13th century. Until the middle of the 18th century, bullfighting was considered an event for aristocrats, but under the influence of Philip V of Anjou, it became the widely popular event it remains today.

The rules were fixed in the 18th century and have not changed since. But the matador — the killer of the bull — has now been transformed into the torero — an artful performer whose intricate maneuvers symbolize the eternal struggle between man and the wild animal.

**ABOVE FAR LEFT** *Certain posters, announcing bullfights and depicting famous matadors, who have taken on roles similar to those of movie stars, are rare today.*

**ABOVE LEFT** *A 30-foot-high cutout bull-shaped billboard advertising a brand of port wine is a familiar sight along roads in the south.*

**CENTER FAR LEFT, CENTER LEFT, AND RIGHT** *Seville's Plaza de Toros or bullfight arena, like most of the others, has seats that range from the least expensive and sweltering* sol, *or sun, to the most costly and comfortable,* sombra, *or shade.*

**FAR LEFT** *The bull motif also appears as a door knocker in Estremadura.*

**LEFT** *The vast Plaza de Toros in Barcelona was built in 1900 in the fashionable Moorish style by the architect August Font i Carreras.*

CORRIDA de TOROS

Al campo.

Suerte de vara.

Preparando para matar.

En el campo

El defile

Suerte de capa.

**LEFT** *A matador is depicted wearing the* traje de luces – *the suit of lights – on a rare series of installment postcards that dates from 1913. Individual postcards would be sent out on successive days, and in this case 10 cards make up the complete puzzlelike image.*

**ABOVE** *A vintage postcard – a black-and-white photograph with gold embroidery – portrays the matador Camara.*

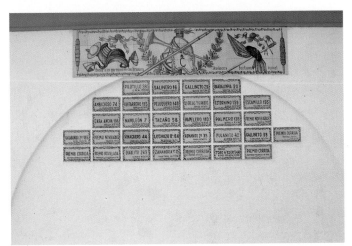

**LEFT AND RIGHT** *The Cortijo San Andres, near Seville, belongs to Salvador Sanchez Barbudo and his wife, Carmen, and specializes in training horses. The cortijo, or farmhouse, dates from the 17th century. The meticulously kept stables and training rings are witness to the continuing traditions for which the area is known.*

14

# CHAPTER

## 2

# LIVING IN SPAIN

In most countries, economic and technological developments have led to the neglect and disappearance of many aspects of a traditional way of life.

But in Spain, a slower economic pace and a strong hold on old-fashioned values have helped keep much of the past intact. There are still numerous small workshops where craftsmen make pottery, papier-mâché, and tinware; old stores where fans, sombreros, and mantillas bespeak a colorful past; and atmospheric cafes, where people get together as in the time of their grandparents.

**ABOVE** *Luis Domenéch i Montaner interpreted Saint Paul in mosaic tile in the Barcelona hospital that was built between 1902 and 1912 and is dedicated to the saint.*

**RIGHT** *A Baroque church and medieval castle dominate one of the humble white villages of Andalusia.*

16

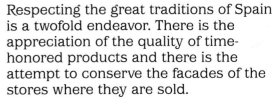

Respecting the great traditions of Spain is a twofold endeavor. There is the appreciation of the quality of time-honored products and there is the attempt to conserve the facades of the stores where they are sold.

Many such emporiums still exist — in the Barri Gótic, or Gothic Quarter, of Barcelona, along the winding streets of Madrid's Malasana area, and in cities from Seville to Segovia where the past is still very much part of the present.

**LEFT, BELOW, AND RIGHT** *Shops in Madrid, Barcelona, and Seville – all with old facades and well-ordered arrays of goods – offer such wares as shiny aluminum pots and pans, perfume, candies, and baby clothes, as well as fans and sombreros.*

**LEFT** *An herbalist's shop in Barcelona, a sombrero shop in Seville, a candy store in Madrid, a boutique for Andalusian dresses in Seville, a shop selling religious objects, and a grocery in Barcelona display a panoply of vintage interiors.*

**RIGHT** *In Barcelona, a store is stocked with glass objects, including colorful and traditional porróns.*

**BELOW RIGHT** *The basement of El Ingenio, on the Calle Raurich in Barcelona, has shelves filled with the giant papier-mâché masks and figures used in religious festivals and for theatrical productions.*

**LEFT** *Canvas awnings, such as these over a narrow street in Seville, are drawn at midday to provide relief from the sun.*

**TOP** *The glass-enclosed dining room by the architect Oscar Tusquets at Azulete, one of Barcelona's most fashionable restaurants, has a series of striped sunshades to modulate the dazzling afternoon light.*

**ABOVE** *Called Umbracle, the cast-iron columned and wood-framed open structure in Barcelona's Parque de la Ciutadella, an 1884 work by Josep Fontsere i Mestres, is a unique greenhouse that offers an oasis of shade.*

Cafes welcome Spaniards at any time during the day or night, whether in city *galerías,* along the sidewalk, filling the Plaza Mayor — main plaza — or overlooking the port. In the morning it's *café con leche.* By one P.M., a glass of wine with tapas, small finger foods or appetizers that change according to the region — squid and cheese in Galicia, fried fish in Andalusia, tortillas in all of Spain. After work, at about seven P.M., it is time for the *merienda;* hot chocolate and maybe some cold cuts are consumed. Dinner is later, beginning after ten P.M..

**LEFT**   *Due to the generally temperate weather, people congregate at cafes set up with tables and chairs outside for most of the year. But during the summer, especially on the islands of Minorca and Mallorca, one may linger for hours and watch the world go by.*

**RIGHT**   *The interiors of the larger cafes and wine bars have an atmosphere all their own. Multicolored tiles line the walls of a cafe in Seville, while the high-ceilinged wood-paneled main room of a cafe on Minorca is a soothing, quiet retreat on a hot midsummer afternoon.*

**TOP, ABOVE, AND RIGHT** *La Taberna del Alcalde, the mayor's tavern, on the village of Pedraza's medieval Plaza Mayor, dates from the middle of the 19th century. The tavern has been owned for more than 50 years by Don Mariano Pascual, who was mayor of the village for 25 years. The original interior of the cafe has never been altered—only smoke has given the walls and furnishings an added patina.*

**ABOVE AND LEFT**  *Like many others, this small, authentic cafe in Seville – with its framed pictures of toreros and posters of famous bullfights – reflects the passion of the owner and his habitués for the corrida.*

# CHAPTER 3

# ELEMENTS OF SPANISH STYLE

Hispano-Moorish architecture, Christian architecture, the Renaissance, the Baroque, Neoclassicism, and Catalan *modernismo* are highlights in the diversity of architectural styles that characterize Spain and reflect its complex history of foreign invasions and influences.

Spain's stylistic diversity can be seen in such design elements as shaded patios, romantic miradors or balconies, dramatic spires, textured walls, and imposing doors.

**ABOVE**  Azulejos – *glazed tiles – decorate the wall below a double Mudejar-style arch in Seville's Alcazar.*

**RIGHT**  *The rooftops and spires of Seville's Gothic cathedral contrast with the classical 18th-century Archivo de Indias, where more than 30,000 documents relating to the discovery of America are stored.*

**LEFT AND RIGHT** *The spires, belfries, and domes that typify traditional Spanish architecture have their origins in the Islamic buildings of Moorish Spain: the clock tower at left, in Barcelona, with its lacy iron cupola sheltering a family of storks, was inspired by minarets. Some of the most memorable examples include Baroque motifs as well. Enlivened with gargoyles, obelisks, columns, and finials, these landmarks, particularly Antonio Gaudí's Sagrada Familia cathedral in Barcelona (top row, center right), are dramatic and enduring focal points of the changing cityscape.*

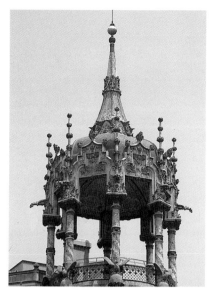

**LEFT AND RIGHT** *In Spain, a blank wall seems to have always been seen as an opportunity for decoration. Few countries in Europe offer such a rich diversity of textures, colors, and materials in the embellishment of building facades. Even the rubble stone of the humble cottages that line a hilly street in Pollensa on the island of Mallorca are distinguished by smooth stone doors and window frames.*

*By contrast, the riotous tile mosaic that covers the whole surface of an apartment house, or flamboyant Gothic reliefs, or carved stone umbrellas and fans of Japanese inspiration, as well as black-and-white chevrons, or ocher stucco inlaid with tile – all express the imaginative and colorful approach to the fanciful in building.*

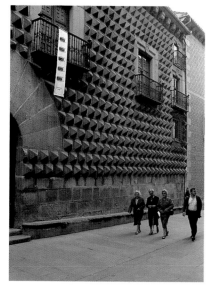

34

**LEFT AND RIGHT** *From Cáceres in the Estremadura region in the west to the region of Catalonia in the east, to Andalusia in the south, the walls of Spain, painted with bright frescoes, emblazoned with carved stone coats of arms, or even revealing mud bricks beneath crumbling stucco, recall a history of cultural diversity.*

**LEFT** *The noble and historic doorways of Spanish houses turn entering a building into a ceremony. Doors – whether studded with cast-brass nails, or protected by wrought-iron grillework and framed with fluted columns and broken pediments – offer a grand if not necessarily warm welcome.*

**RIGHT** *In Córdoba, an interior portal takes the form of a Baroque archway.*

**LEFT AND RIGHT** *The mirador, or enclosed overhanging balcony, is a ubiquitous feature of residential Spanish architecture. Because of the long-standing practice of secluding women in Spain (similar to that in Islamic countries) these balconies created a vantage point from which women could look out, and in some cases be seen, while still remaining apart from the outside world.*

*Today, the glass-enclosed structures, often boasting a delicate iron framework or decorated with sinuous scrollwork, provide a sunny place to display plants and keep an eye on the activities in the street below.*

40

**LEFT** *All over Spain but especially in the south, courtyards, filled with orange and palm trees and potted plants, often with a fountain at its center and ringed with ivy-covered columns, are one of the strongest reminders of the influence of Moorish architecture. All the rooms open onto the courtyard or patio, allowing it to function as the center of the house.*

**RIGHT** *The Patio de las Muñecas, in the Alcazar in Seville, is one of the legendary 14th-century palace's numerous courtyards. Organized around a fountain – water played an important part in the Moorish tradition–the patio boasts Islamic capitals and graceful cusped arches.*

**ABOVE** Azulejos *form an unfading street sign in the Estremadura region.*

**LEFT** *Blue, white, and yellow tiles with a Neoclassical pattern of arabesques cover the facade of a turn-of-the-century building in Cáceres.*

**RIGHT** *In Barcelona, yellow and blue tiles depict a stylized Renaissance balustrade topped with pots of blooming plants and bowls of fruit. The vibrant glazed-tile pattern is a popular motif that has been in production since the 17th century.*

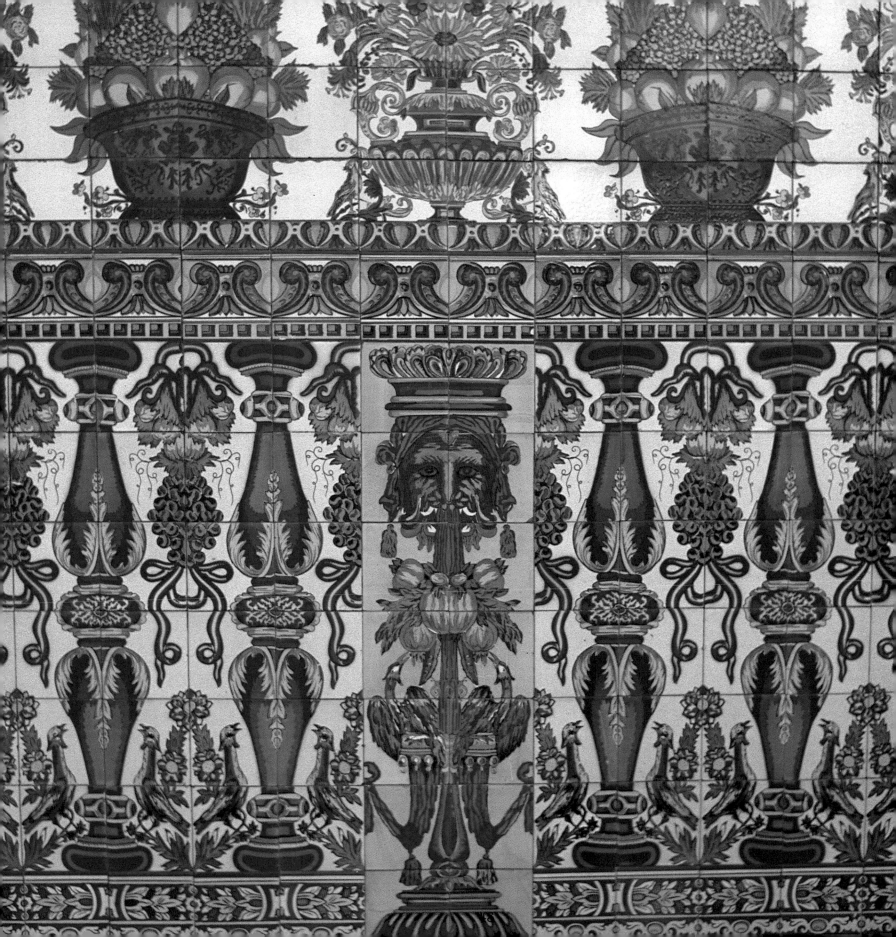

**LEFT** *Undulating over a Baroque dome in Seville, forming a mosaic of broken shards in Antonio Gaudí's sensuous Parc Güell in Barcelona, or creating intricate geometric interlacing or trompe l'oeil patterns, glazed ceramics play an important part in the visual fabric of Spain.*

**RIGHT** *In Madrid, vintage tiled facades are charming advertisements for a poultry and egg vendor, and for a pharmacy that touts a black tea with cleansing powers.*

**LEFT AND RIGHT** *The Casa Thomas, at 291 Calle de Mallorca in Barcelona, is a stunning example of the work of Luis Domenéch i Montaner and was built between 1895 and 1898. The ground-floor foyer reflects the influence of Catalan modernismo on all the applied arts in architecture: ceramic tile, glass, iron, wood, and stone. Every surface and detail is richly ornamented with floral, animal, or fruit motifs – including the exquisite pomegranate, a detail of the stained-glass window on the landing.*

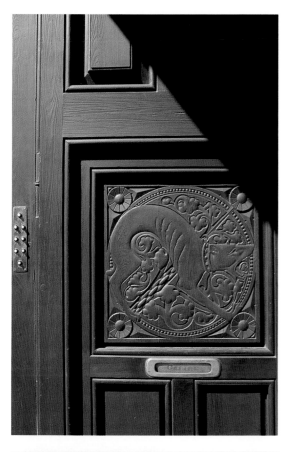

ABOVE, ABOVE LEFT, LEFT, AND RIGHT   *Once a private home – called the Casa Lleo i Morera and designed by Domenéch i Montaner in 1903 – the residence, situated at 25 Passeig de Gracia, now houses the Patronato Municipal de Turismo de Barcelona, the city's municipal tourist board.*

*Carles Bassó and Oscar Tusquets renovated the building. The interior, whose decorations and furnishings were originally coordinated by Gaspar Homar, has been restored by Mireia Riera. The flamboyant and spectacular ornamentations in stained glass, mosaic tile, and carved wood – including the doorframes that depict a Catalan fable as well as floral and bird motifs and charming and intricately detailed bucolic scenes – offer a rare view of* modernismo *on an intimate scale.*

# CHAPTER 4

# SPANISH ACCENTS

Spain is a country where widely diversified landscapes and a tumultuous history have had a direct influence on architectural styles.

A palace of aristocratic lineage on an island, an apartment of typically Spanish taste bordering on kitsch, an avant-garde interpretation of Catalan *modernismo*, a bourgeois residence, not without nostalgia, in Madrid, a vast Andalusian *cortijo* where a family dynasty still lives on its lands, cultivating olives and raising bulls and horses, and a historical jewel of a house, an early masterpiece by the Catalan architect Antonio Gaudí i Cornet — each is, in its own way, part of this heritage.

**ABOVE** *The influence of the geometric Mudejar style is reflected in the facade of a 19th-century apartment building in Andalusia.*

**RIGHT** *A small village is nestled in the mountains near Avila.*

## GRAND GESTURES

Duarte Pinto Coelho, a famous international interior decorator, lives in a luxurious apartment in the Pinohermosa Palace on the Calle San Pedro in Madrid.

Although the rooms are of princely proportions — the music room is 60 feet long, the dining room 27 feet long — the decorator has managed to create an environment that is grand without being forbidding.

Silk damask draperies, comfortable sofas and easy chairs, rugs layered one atop the other, and Pinto Coelho's eclectic collections — from Chinese Export porcelain to Renaissance bronzes — are artfully united through skillful treatments of texture and color.

**ABOVE FAR LEFT, AND FAR LEFT** *The apartment is located on the second floor of Madrid's Pinohermosa Palace, a grand mansion now divided into spacious apartments. The "marble" stairwell is actually trompe l'oeil.*

**ABOVE LEFT AND LEFT** *The service hall near the kitchen also displays and stores Duarte Pinto Coelho's impressive collection of china.*

**RIGHT** *The 17-century Spanish trompe l'oeil and gilt organ is the focus of the large music room.*

**LEFT** *Decorative objects are grouped on tables and consoles – including Italian bronzes, Chinese porcelain, and classical busts. An antique Japanese screen and 17th-century Dutch tiled stove enrich the decor.*

**RIGHT** *Duarte Pinto Coelho divided the enormous living room into a few intimate seating areas.*

**ABOVE** *An immense Portuguese rug stretches from one end of the 27-foot-long dining room to the other. The walls and ceiling have been painted in trompe l'oeil.*

**ABOVE** *Sparkling silver serving pieces are displayed in cabinets in a tile-lined room off the kitchen.*

**ABOVE**   The small salon is decorated in the spirit of the 19th century, with vibrant red wallpaper and comfortable chairs and sofas.

**RIGHT**   Stone columns with gilded capitals edge the front of the 19th-century Neoclassical mahogany bookcase in the salon.

**FAR RIGHT**   Above an antique ebony desk are displayed a collection of French paintings on glass.

**ABOVE LEFT AND LEFT**
*The rich embroidered fabric
of the half-tester bed, the
ornamental painting of the
bedroom door, and the marqueterie patterns of the floor
give a harmonious feeling
to the master bedroom.*

**ABOVE** *In the boudoir-
bathroom, a Realist portrait
of the interior decorator
hangs above the marble tub.*

## HOUSE AND GARDEN

Alfabia — the name comes from an Arabic word meaning large earthenware jar — an estate on the island of Mallorca, sits in a luxuriant Moorish-style garden extending over the warm south-facing slopes of a mountain. The stucco house, which appears to be a 17th-century seignorial residence, was originally built by Arabs in the 1300s. Except for the vaulted ceiling of the porch and the geometric plan of the garden, few 14th-century elements remain.

Baroque architectural embellishments contrast with the austere facades. On the interior, exceptional collections of heirlooms from the 17th to the early 19th century are enhanced by the simplicity and scale of the rooms.

**ABOVE**   *The two-faced Roman god Janus decorates a slender column on the courtyard doorway.*

**ABOVE FAR LEFT**   *The weathered facade has Baroque curves. The rounded gable, arched entrance, and oval windows all date from the 17th century.*

**FAR LEFT**   *Water can still be drawn from the old well in the garden.*

**LEFT**   *The groin vault of the low entrance porch dates from the 1300s.*

**ABOVE AND RIGHT**   *At the center of the cobblestone-paved courtyard an old plane tree shades an octagonal fountain with a statue of a boy with a dolphin. The tree sits in a green island of potted plants surrounded by a curve of volcanic stones.*

**TOP AND LEFT** *The tiled entrance gallery has a low barrel vault and rows of early 18th-century hall benches carved with the family's coat of arms. Above one hangs a painting of a stalking jaguar.*

**ABOVE AND RIGHT** *The beamed library is not only a repository for old volumes bound in calfskin but also contains early 17th-century chairs and rare Spanish architectural engravings.*

**TOP** *An equestrian portrait painted in 1666 nearly fills a wall of the grand salon. The floor is covered in beige ceramic tile.*

**ABOVE AND RIGHT** *The wainscoting in the salon is painted with landscapes representing the villages of Mallorca interspersed with Rococo flourishes. The rest of the walls have been covered with a blue-and-white patterned fabric that is also used for the door valances. A gold-and-vermilion wooden chandelier hangs from the beamed ceiling. The 17th-century chest is covered with silk and studded with brass nails in a decorative design.*

**ABOVE AND ABOVE RIGHT**
*The walls of the small salon are hung with yellow silk damask above the wainscoting painted with landscape scenes. The unsophisticated carved mantelpiece is juxtaposed with the gilded mirror and the splendid gold-and-white Rococo French door on the opposite wall.*

**ABOVE** *A series of green-shuttered windows opens onto a raised and tiled veranda that is enveloped with wisteria.*

**ABOVE, ABOVE RIGHT, AND RIGHT**
*A vaulted gallery with a colonnade and grandiose stairways overgrown with semitropical vegetation lead to the famed gardens of Alfabia.*

**ABOVE LEFT, ABOVE, AND LEFT**
*Pairs of recumbent lions, columns, and benches along with double rows of palm trees help to form a strong, symmetrical architectural framework among the unruly tangle of plants.*

## LIVING MUSEUM

Pura Ortí Pastor, a painter, lives in the old part of Ibiza's Dalt Vila, or Upper Town, a medieval fortified town that is today a busy tourist attraction.

In the 1950s, Pastor and her husband, Ignacio Agudo Clará (also a painter), moved into the apartment, which was once part of the Palacio Bardaji, a formerly grand 17th-century palace that had fallen into disrepair.

Since her husband died nearly 25 years ago, Pastor has been the guardian of his paintings and of the place where he lived and worked.

**ABOVE**  *Pura Ortí Pastor sits at the dining room table in her Ibiza home.*

**ABOVE LEFT AND LEFT**  *Plants in pots are kept on one of the balconies.*

**RIGHT**  *The near absence of furniture in the living room permits the paintings by Ignacio Agudo Clará to dominate the understated interior.*

70

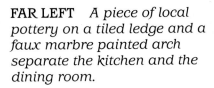

FAR LEFT   *A piece of local pottery on a tiled ledge and a faux marbre painted arch separate the kitchen and the dining room.*

LEFT   *The dining suite has been in the same place since Ortí Pastor and her husband moved into the apartment.*

BELOW FAR LEFT   *The study is filled with personal memorabilia.*

BELOW LEFT   *In the dining room, Ortí Pastor has created a still life in memory of her husband. Under one of his self-portraits are his palette, the violin he played as a child, and a bronze escutcheon of Richard Wagner, Agudo Clará's favorite composer.*

RIGHT AND BELOW
RIGHT   *In the modest white-tiled kitchen, meats are cooked on a simple hotplate. A piece of flowered oilcloth covers the table.*

BELOW FAR RIGHT   *A crucifix hangs above the bed in the plain small bedroom.*

74

# GAUDI REVISITED

A few years ago, Fernando Amat, the owner of Vinçón, Barcelona's most influential modern home furnishings store, had the opportunity to move to one of the last original apartments in Casa Milá.

The Catalan architect Antonio Gaudí designed the apartment building known as La Pedrera — the Quarry. Completed in 1910 on the Passeig de Gracia, it is now one of the city's most important landmarks of *modernismo*.

While Amat has respected the apartment's traditional layout and celebrated its curved walls, original doors and windows, and unusual proportions, he has been able to express his avant-garde point of view simply by repainting in bold colors and dotting the rooms with art and furniture by leading international designers and artists.

**LEFT**   *Gaudí conceived of La Pedrera, now a historic landmark, as an organic structure. The 1910 facade was recently cleaned.*

**ABOVE RIGHT**   *The wrought-iron entrance gate resembles a huge spider web, further enhancing the naturalistic theme of the overall design.*

**ABOVE FAR RIGHT**   *Fernando Amat and his dog, Milou, stand on the roof garden of the building where the chimneys are covered in a mosaic of white marble and ceramic.*

**RIGHT**   *In the courtyard, the glass doors have been decorated in a sandblasted flower pattern.*

**LEFT**   With Carlos Riart, a Catalan architect and furniture designer, as a consultant, Fernando Amat painted the circular corridor and its organic moldings, door, and window frames a bright green.

**BELOW FAR LEFT**   In the corridor, Elizabeth Garouste and Mattia Bonetti's 1981 patinated iron and ponyskin Barbarian chair is displayed near a 1973 table by Bigas Luna. The lamp by Isamu Noguchi is made of cast iron, bamboo, and silk. The 1975 painting is by Angel Jové, a contemporary artist.

**BELOW LEFT**   A 1950s armchair faces a 1988 painting by Francesca Llopis. The artwork leaning against the wall is a Mona Lisa by Angel Planells, a Surrealist painter who was a contemporary of Salvador Dali.

**RIGHT**   Also along the corridor stand a lamp of unknown origin, made of three zebra legs, and a 1981 prototype of the Gairo chair by Mariscal.

**ABOVE** In the living room, undulating walls are painted dark blue and the parquet floors are original. Fernando Amat has created an homage to Gaudí, placing a reedition of Gaudí's Calvet stool on an aluminum platform fitted with casters.

**LEFT** The door between the dining room and one of the bedrooms has been painted to contrast with the blue wall.

**RIGHT** A velvet-covered banquette hugs a corner of the living room.

**ABOVE** *Lighting by the German designer Ingo Maurer hangs over the dining table. The table as well as the red-and-green velvet arm-chairs are by Carlos Riart.*

**LEFT** *The living room has access to a long, narrow balcony, which is ringed with a twisted wrought-iron banister by Gaudí.*

**RIGHT** *The simply furnished master bedroom is off the dining room.*

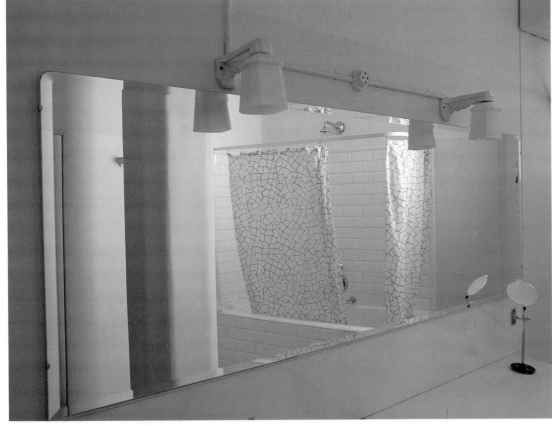

**ABOVE LEFT AND LEFT**  *Very few changes were made to the high-ceilinged, white-tiled master bathroom. Fernando Amat chose to retain the old-fashioned fixtures, including a pull-chain toilet.*

**ABOVE**  *A lamp by Ingo Maurer stands on a white linen cloth embroidered in homage to the artist Marcel Duchamp.*

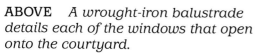

**ABOVE** *A wrought-iron balustrade details each of the windows that open onto the courtyard.*

**ABOVE RIGHT AND RIGHT** *Although new appliances were installed in the kitchen, the vintage look of the room, with its glass-fronted cabinets and biomorphic window, was retained.*

# AMERICAN DIPLOMACY

Shortly after arriving in Spain in 1945, the American Harris H. Williams moved into an apartment in this building in Madrid, where he has lived ever since. Now retired from years of diplomatic service, he continues to collect Spanish furniture and artworks.

The apartment mirrors the life of a sensitive person who has surrounded himself with meaningful objects — some very personal, others telling of a refined and original sense of esthetics.

**ABOVE FAR LEFT**  *The highly polished old-fashioned elevator still has its beveled glass door.*

**BELOW FAR LEFT**  *The front door opens directly onto the corridor.*

**ABOVE LEFT**  *The living room is an unusual combination of 19th-century paintings, Moderne furniture, and a classical bust.*

**LEFT AND RIGHT**  *The faux marbre table is the focus of the dining room. Silver serving pieces are arranged on a carved and painted console. The 1950s steel-frame chairs are upholstered in yellow velvet.*

**LEFT** *The round convex mirror with its gilded sunburst frame hangs over the mantelpiece in the library.*

**RIGHT** *The table in the living room incorporates the signs of the zodiac.*

**CENTER RIGHT** *An Old Master painting is centered over the wood mantel in the dining room.*

**FAR RIGHT** *Ava Gardner, the movie actress, dedicated a photograph to her friend Harris H. Williams.*

**BELOW RIGHT** *Majolica pitchers and a large religious painting give the hall a traditional Spanish feeling.*

**BELOW CENTER RIGHT** *Ceramic fruits as well as a tureen and asparagus holder are laid out on a small table in the dining room.*

**FAR RIGHT** *Joan Miró, the celebrated Catalan artist, gave the series of whistles, made in a Mallorcan folk art technique, to Williams.*

## HOSPITABLE HACIENDA

A few miles from the Andalusian city of Seville, on the road to Cádiz, stands the Hacienda de Bujalmoro, surrounded by fields of cotton. Although the main part of the hacienda was completed in the 17th century, some elements date from the 13th century.

Originally owned by the powerful Minacelli family, the estate is now the property of Juan Ibara, a manufacturer of a leading olive oil.

The olives are grown, picked, sorted, pressed, and packed on the estate. Although Ibara and his family do not live full-time at the hacienda, the industrialist often travels from Seville to visit there.

**ABOVE**   *The 13th-century mirador, or tower, overlooks the inner courtyard, the oldest part of the hacienda, and the olive groves behind.*

**RIGHT**   *The facade is in the Baroque style typical of Sevillan architecture of the late 17th century.*

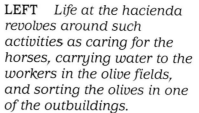

**LEFT** *Life at the hacienda revolves around such activities as caring for the horses, carrying water to the workers in the olive fields, and sorting the olives in one of the outbuildings.*

**RIGHT AND BELOW RIGHT** *The windows indicate Arab influence, already established in this area by the 13th century.*

**BOTTOM RIGHT** *At one end of the covered patio, a panel of 18th-century tiles has been set into the wall under the Minacelli coat of arms.*

**ABOVE**  *The long, narrow corridor runs the width of the main house and ends in a private garden.*

**ABOVE RIGHT**  *The living room is furnished with comfortable easy chairs upholstered in chintz.*

**RIGHT**  *A rush carpet covers the terracotta tiled floor in which a number of* azulejos *have been inserted.*

90

**ABOVE AND ABOVE LEFT** *The dark wood furniture, formal family portraits, and bare tile floor contribute to the severe look of the reception rooms.*

**LEFT** *A grille-covered window overlooks the private chapel.*

**ABOVE** *The entrance to the 17th-century private chapel is framed in Moorish azulejos.*

**ABOVE AND RIGHT**
*The gilt-decorated Baroque altarpiece and tile-lined walls of the private chapel are typically Spanish.*

# VISIONARY VILLA

Situated on the Calle de los Carolinas in Barcelona's Gracia district, the Casa Viçens, a private residence, was built between 1884 and 1885 for Manuel Viçens, a manufacturer of ceramic tile. The house was the first realized residential commission by Antonio Gaudí, the renowned Catalan architect whose visionary and individual modernist work was a Spanish counterpart to the English Arts and Crafts movement.

Before it was completed, the house was sold to the Jover family. Fabiola Jover de Herrero and her husband, a doctor, still live there. Although some modifications were made to the house in the 1920s, it remains an important historic monument, representing a turning point in the development of *modernismo.*

**LEFT, ABOVE RIGHT, AND ABOVE FAR RIGHT** *The facade of the Casa Viçens is entirely covered in ceramic tile, a Hispano-Moorish feature favored by Gaudí. The front gate's grillework in the shape of palmetto fronds is a tour-de-force of hand-wrought iron.*

**RIGHT AND FAR RIGHT** *A large majolica urn on an iron tripod has as its backdrop a wall of stone and tile.*

**ABOVE** *The ceiling of the vestibule borrows its motifs from nature and Arab architecture.*

**ABOVE** *Graceful palm fronds painted on the ceiling of the veranda give the illusion of a garden canopy.*

**ABOVE** *A 19th-century Catalan artist, F. Torres Cassana, painted the seascapes and landscapes in the dining room.*

**ABOVE** *Cutout birds and leaves fly around above painted panels depicting cranes in the deep window recesses that face the veranda. The tilework on the fireplace is Moorish in influence.*

**TOP, ABOVE, AND RIGHT**    *In the dining room, the spaces between the wood ceiling beams have been cast in plaster in deep relief in an intricate olive branch design. The built-in cabinets enframing oil paintings were conceived by Antonio Gaudí as part of the room's original scheme of decoration.*

# CHAPTER 5

# THE PALACE

Throughout Spain there are cathedrals, monasteries, and castles that illustrate the eclectic styles of Spanish architecture — along with palaces that mirror their grandeur and majesty.

The residences of wealthy aristocratic families, multiwinged palaces were organized around arcaded patios and surrounded by well-tended gardens dotted with fountains. While few and far between, the palaces that remain still function somewhat as they did in the past — but not without the effort and expense that such grand residences require.

**ABOVE**  *A detail of the facade of the Casa Gremial Dels Velers o de la Seda in Barcelona is an elegant example of 18th-century Catalan decoration.*

**RIGHT**  *Segovia's Alcazar castle appears like a mirage at the edge of a field of high grasses.*

## PRIVATE MUSEUM

Francisco Godia, a lawyer, and his wife, Inés, live in a mansion that was built in the 14th century by Franciscan monks as a guest house for the monastery of Pedralbes. Once a country village, Pedralbes is now considered a suburb of Barcelona.

In the spacious house, Godia has continued to assemble the remarkable collections of museum-quality artworks that were begun by his father. In addition to decorative objects — earthenware and ceramics, religious art from the Middle Ages, Oriental carpets, and ceramic tiles from the 15th to the 19th century — Godia has collected spectacular paintings by early 20th-century artists such as Ramon Casas, José Gusachs, José Gutierrez Solona, Torres Garcia, Juan Gris, and Pablo Picasso.

**FAR LEFT AND ABOVE LEFT**  *A marble sculpture by Josep Maria Subirachs, a contemporary Catalan artist, is on the front lawn.*

**BELOW LEFT**  *Grass grows wild on the wide steps in the terraced side garden.*

**ABOVE, ABOVE RIGHT, AND RIGHT**  *Palm trees, giant ferns, and luxuriant vines create a near-tropical garden in the patio.*

**ABOVE**   *In a corner of the hall, an 18th-century putto is the base of a table, which supports a marble tabletop, which in turn holds an antique Chinese porcelain jar. The chairs are 18th-century French.*

**ABOVE RIGHT**   *Pointed, vaulted arches surround the center hall.*

**RIGHT**   *An impressive collection of small earthenware holy water fonts from Catalonia, Mallorca, and Valencia and dating from the 16th to the 18th century decorate the entrance walls to the private chapel.*

**ABOVE, ABOVE LEFT, AND LEFT** *The walls of the courtyard are studded with hundreds of tiles that were made in the 16th to the 19th century in Toledo, Seville, and Valencia.*

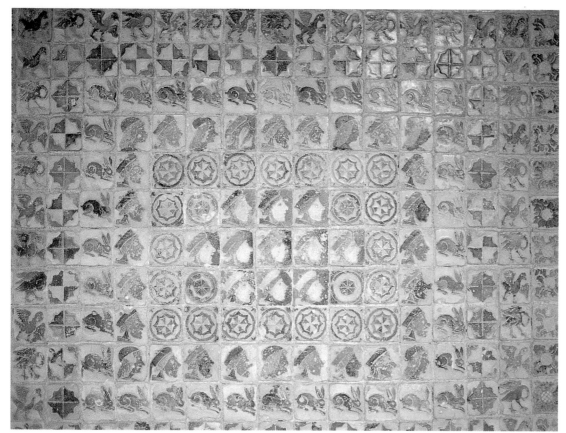

**FAR LEFT**  *A 15th-century Flemish polyptych, a large medieval book of hymns, a 14th-century Spanish wrought-iron church candelabrum, and an antique carpet from Cuenca have been assembled as the focal point in the vaulted-ceilinged corridor.*

**LEFT**  *A Romanesque portal opens onto the drawing room, where polychrome religious statues and paintings line the walls.*

**BELOW LEFT**  *Two 13th-century carved polychrome figures from the León region frame the steps to the library.*

RIGHT *In the corner of the library where he has placed his writing table, Francisco Godia has grouped family photographs, a bronze bust of his father, his car-racing trophies, and, on the wall, an enviable collection of Old Master drawings.*

**ABOVE AND RIGHT** *The formal dining room is furnished with a set of 18th-century Catalan chairs. Glass-fronted vitrines filled with 14th- to 19th-century utilitarian ceramics from Valencia, Aragon, and Catalonia surround the coffered-ceilinged room.*

## ILLUSTRIOUS LEGACY

The Palacio Moxo, begun in the 16th century, stands in the heart of Barcelona's Barri Gòtic, where many buildings date from the 13th to the 15th century.

Saint Ignatius Loyola, founder of the Society of Jesus, or Jesuit order of priests, sojourned here on the way to Santiago de Compostela and supposedly performed a miracle in giving back the owner of the palace his sight. The Moxo family acquired the property in the 18th century and enlarged the *palacio*. The interior has been unchanged since a member of the family refurbished the rooms in the 19th century. The palace now belongs to the Marquise de San Mori, who has lived there for decades, respectful of its heritage.

**ABOVE AND RIGHT**  *The rooms of the house open onto an interior courtyard, converted into a private garden. The decorations in sgraffito on the walls date from the 18th century.*

**ABOVE** *A 16th-century ivory-inlaid Spanish desk in the Renaissance style and a star-shaped processional lantern furnish the foyer.*

**LEFT** *The ornamentation of the two-tone 18th-century facade is sgraffito, white plaster designs scratched to reveal the dark ground underneath.*

ABOVE *The parquet floor and pier mirror of the music room can be glimpsed behind the silk damask draperies.*

**LEFT, BELOW FAR LEFT, AND BELOW LEFT** *The small drawing room, decorated in the 19th century in the French taste of the 18th century, is a suitable setting for the grand array of Charles IV furniture.*

**ABOVE** *The chairs and tables in the game room are Charles IV in style.*

**RIGHT** *The gallerylike formal dining room with its arcaded windows is a reproduction of the royal dining room of King Alfonso XII.*

**RIGHT** *Gilt and brocade-covered chairs are lined up in the damask-walled fairytale music room.*

**ABOVE AND LEFT** *In the music room, the extraordinary gigantic chandelier that hangs from the Italianate painted ceiling, torchères, and the candelabra are all of Baccarat crystal.*

**ABOVE** *The bedroom suite of the Marquise de San Mori includes an adjacent boudoir. The gilt and beveled-glass partition is typically Catalan.*

**RIGHT** *The pair of brilliant Baccarat chandeliers in the drawing room were electrified at the beginning of the century.*

RIGHT *Collections of leather-bound books fill the floor-to-ceiling glass-fronted bookcases in the stately library.*

## MOORISH MEMORIES

The Palacio de la Condesa de Lebrija, today the private home of the Marquise de Meritos and her husband, Eduardo Leone, is one of Seville's grandest residences.

The palace was built in the 16th century in the Mudejar style, with three spacious patios, monumental staircase decorated with *azulejos,* and *artesonados* or coffered ceilings.

In the 19th century, one of the ancestors of the family affirmed his taste for Roman antiquities by installing mosaic floors in the patios and on the ground floor. He also collected Roman busts and a multitude of archaeological finds. The living quarters on the second floor are still decorated as they were at the end of the 19th century.

The Oriental boudoir or smoking room reflects both its authentic Moorish past and the revival style popular in the 19th century.

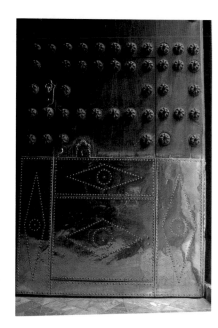

**ABOVE LEFT** *The elaborate stonework at the front entrance contrasts with the brick walls that are painted burnt orange.*

**ABOVE FAR LEFT AND LEFT** *The arcaded patio combines Mudejar cusped arches with an imposing ancient Roman marble mosaic pavement.*

**ABOVE** *The massive front door is ornamented with iron studs and a wide tooled-brass kickguard.*

**RIGHT** *A late Roman bust is displayed against the colorful backdrop of tiles with an arabesque design.*

**ABOVE** *The majestic staircase with high wainscoting and twisted mahogany balusters is supported on shallow vaults.*

**ABOVE** *A bronze bust provides a dramatic focal point on the landing.*

**ABOVE AND ABOVE RIGHT**
*A series of anterooms
in the Neoclassical style of
the 19th century leads to the
drawing room.*

**FAR LEFT** *The domed octagonal-shaped hall is cooled by a fountain playing in a shallow pool surrounded by Roman mosaics.*

**LEFT** *The gallery is lined with glass-fronted cabinets filled with archaeological artifacts.*

**BELOW LEFT** *In the anteroom to the patio, a group of refined early Fernandino furniture stands before three pedimented windows framed by a pair of Ionic columns.*

**RIGHT** *The Roman torso set into a large niche is one of the masterpieces of the collection.*

**ABOVE** *The lunette of a second-floor window has alternating panes of clear and blue glass.*

**LEFT** *A narrow paneled passageway is furnished with English-influenced 18th-century Spanish chairs, ancestral portraits, and other heirlooms.*

**ABOVE RIGHT** *In the dining room, the delicate Fernandino architecture and chandelier blend with the 17th-century–style chairs.*

**RIGHT** *The library, with brilliant scarlet velvet draperies and walls and time-mellowed books, exemplifies mid–19th century Isabelino style.*

**LEFT**  *Decorated in scarlet, crimson, and gold, with silk velvet upholstery and brocaded draperies, the drawing room is a classic example of the Spanish taste for splendor. Old Master paintings of saints, fantastic Baroque pelmets, vitrines of porcelain, and Rococo Revival chandeliers create a luxurious environment.*

**RIGHT**  *The boudoir or smoking room on the second floor has been furnished in the neo-Moorish style favored in the 19th century.*

## STYLISH CONQUEST

Duarte Pinto Coelho's Palacio de los Chaves Mendoza in Trujillo rivals in scale the palaces of the conquistadors for which the medieval town in Estremadura is legendary.

Begun in the 13th century, the building was for several centuries the residence of the Chaves Mendoza family before becoming a Franciscan convent and subsequently the Antiguo Hospital de la Concepción. Since 1979, it has been Pinto Coelho's country home. The interior decorator had spent most of the previous decade renovating its many rooms.

Surprisingly, the palace is grand without being ostentatious. Pinto Coelho has assembled innumerable pieces of furniture and many different collections of objects without losing either his sense of refinement or his taste for authenticity.

**ABOVE LEFT** *Orange trees grow on the garden terraces.*

**LEFT** *A belltower tops the whitewashed facade. Over the door are inset the coats of arms of Spanish grandees.*

**ABOVE** *One of the 17 bedrooms has a terrace with a view of the rose garden and the medieval town of Trujillo.*

**ABOVE RIGHT** *From the palace, the valley stretches out below the fortifications of the town.*

**RIGHT** *A well stands in the courtyard, which is filled with luxuriant plants.*

LEFT   A pair of 17th-century polychrome wood-statue torchères welcomes visitors to the palace.

BELOW LEFT   The open patio with its tall stone arches is a cloistered retreat.

RIGHT   In the recesses of the patio, Duarte Pinto Coelho has arranged a collection of painted and stripped-pine country furniture and folk art.

**LEFT** *At every turn, in every corner, up the stairs and on the landings, as well as along the gallery above the patio, Duarte Pinto Coelho has placed an intriguing arrangement of objects that range from a wall full of straw hats to a collection of reliquaries in the shape of arms and hands.*

**RIGHT** *The vaulted-ceilinged summer dining room is on the ground floor adjacent to the cool patio. The plates on the wall are from Puente del Arzobispo, a town near Toledo.*

**BELOW RIGHT** *The small sitting room on the second floor has been decorated in a 19th-century style. The colored prints and extraordinary terra-cotta statuettes, matadors and toreadors on horseback, are displayed on and around the multitiered fireplace.*

**ABOVE AND LEFT**  *A garniture of antique Chinese porcelain vases lines up on the mantelpiece before a plaster relief portrait of Philip V in the vast main drawing room. The interior decorator has arranged the predominantly French and Spanish furniture in 19th-century English style in intimate groupings.*

**LEFT**  *On the ground floor, a small reception room has been turned into a cozy, intimate study.*

**RIGHT**  *On the table in the study is a careful composition of ornamental straw boxes, cigarette cases, and small chests that are as rare as they are delicate.*

## CHAPTER 6

# FAMILY TRADITIONS

Even if it becomes necessary to divide the patriarchal home in order to keep it in the family, many old Spanish houses have survived.

While some houses have remained as if untouched by time, others have been adapted to function in a contemporary world; yet all reflect the strong Spanish attachment to the family and to the traditional values that implies.

In the varying styles of the houses — from the intimate world of a poet to the multigenerational *cortijo* — are portrayed the different heritages that have been handed down in the cities, as in the country or on the islands.

**ABOVE**   *A window is protected with a wrought-iron grille, as is customary of many houses in Estremadura.*

**RIGHT**   *In Seville, a patchwork pattern in shades of ocher and white is created by the contrast of the plaster walls and the terra-cotta tiled roofs.*

## PRESERVATION ACT

The 15th-century residence known as the Palacio de los Montero has been in the same family for centuries. Located in the fortified Dalt Vila, or Upper Town, on the island of Ibiza, it has sweeping views of the Mediterranean over the rooftops of the town.

Like most of the more modest homes on the island, the grand house has a whitewashed facade that is in keeping with the traditions of the island. Carlos Riquer, who is in his early twenties, is the heir to this estate. While otherwise a non-conformist, he is committed to preserving the palace in its original state, rather than trying to modernize it and change its character.

**LEFT**  *A cartouche of the family coat of arms decorates the severe facade.*

**FAR LEFT**  *A long balcony at the rear of the palace overlooks the town of Ibiza and the sea.*

**RIGHT, BELOW RIGHT, AND BELOW FAR RIGHT**  *A suite of mid – 19th century Isabelino red silk damask – covered chairs and sofa are the main furnishings of the small salon. A pair of portraits by Ignacio Zuloaga hang on the walls along with a sunny seascape by artist Joaquín Sorolla.*

**TOP, TOP RIGHT, ABOVE, AND ABOVE RIGHT**   *A series of Isabelino chairs inspired by 17th-century English models parade around the walls of the large reception room, below a frieze of family portraits.*

**RIGHT**   *The living room is of baronial proportions. A huge wrought-iron chandelier hangs from the ceiling of varnished wood. Traditional fringed carpets woven in the Balearic Islands barely cover the wide-plank floor that has become bleached from years of scrubbing.*

**ABOVE** *In the dining room, a collection of majolica plates creates a swirling pattern around the provincial Baroque-style cabinets.*

**ABOVE** *Heavy draperies and velvet-upholstered chairs enhance the formality and Old World feeling of the dining room.*

**ABOVE** *The crown atop the silk damask canopy indicates the noble provenance of the late 19th-century brass bed.*

143

## SCULPTURAL FEAT

It was only at the death of her son Ramon in the early 1950s, when she was in her fifties, that Eulalia Fabregas de Sentmenat began her career and became a distinguished sculptor. The self-taught artist has since produced hundreds of masterful Neoclassical works — mostly figures in wood, stone, marble, and bronze.

While many of her pieces are represented in prestigious European private collections and museums, by far the most extensive collection of her work adorns the grounds and interiors of her family's 18th-century Mediterranean-style country residence in Esplugas, near Barcelona.

Statues not only top the balustraded parapet and stand along the edge of the driveway, they also line the entrance hall of the stuccoed villa.

The reception rooms on the second floor remain much as they were 30 years ago. Yet more sculpture, family portraits — some in the glamorous images popular in the 1940s and 1950s — fine antiques and luxurious textiles are combined in stylishly mannered still lifes.

**ABOVE LEFT**  *Statues by Eulalia Fabregas de Sentmenat are dramatically silhouetted against the Mediterranean landscape of cypress and palm trees.*

**LEFT, ABOVE, AND RIGHT**  *The barrel-vaulted hall functions as a gallery for the bronze and marble figures. The only other elements are a 16th-century tapestry and antique sconces.*

ABOVE  Family photographs surround a marble bust of the sculptor Eulalia Fabregas de Sentmenat.

RIGHT  In the drawing room, festooned draperies of satin and chintz, gilded vitrines filled with porcelain, a Savonnerie carpet, and a suite of Louis XVI – inspired furniture recall the mid – 19th century taste in decoration.

**ABOVE** *From the dining room, fringed navy blue and gold brocade draperies partially obscure the view into the drawing room.*

**ABOVE** *A graceful chandelier from the 1830s with alternating branches of candles and electric lights hangs in the dining room.*

**ABOVE** *The hunting theme introduced by a painting depicting dogs attacking a wild boar is carried through by a collection of Staffordshire spaniels and faience birds on the console. Silver and crystal swans and roosters are reflected in the highly polished table.*

**LEFT**  *Isabelino chairs, consoles, and mirrors line the perimeter walls of the wide wood-beamed gallery on the second floor. Antique carpets are dispersed on the wax-polished tile floor.*

**RIGHT**  *Portraits of women in the artist's family dating from three centuries provide focal points in the gallery. A magnificent Venetian glass chandelier, Chinese porcelains, and an opulent Rococo Revival bed are some of the furnishings in the rooms that adjoin the gallery.*

## SUBURBAN ESTATE

At the end of the 19th century, the village of Esplugas — a few miles outside Barcelona — attracted the upper middle class seeking escape from the city's summer heat.

The Casa Mila in Barcelona, one of the masterpieces of *modernismo,* was named after Pablo Mila y Camps, a textile manufacturer who was Antonio Gaudí's patron.

Today, Esplugas is a suburb of Barcelona and the Count and Countess del Montseny and their children live year round in one of the wings of the original stone chalet that was handed down to them.

**ABOVE AND LEFT**   *A bust of the family patriarch is nestled in luxuriant bougainvillea that grows on the facade of the late 19th-century brick chalet.*

**ABOVE RIGHT**   *An Isabelino Rococo Revival mahogany center table is the focus of the entrance hall.*

**ABOVE FAR RIGHT**   *The sitting room, known as the Rotunda, was originally an open veranda. The Art Nouveau Daum vase and circular Aubusson carpet came from France.*

**RIGHT**   *A tapestry depicting the family's coat of arms hangs over a settee in the entrance hall.*

**FAR RIGHT**   *The series of ground-floor reception rooms is separated by curtained glass doors.*

**ABOVE AND LEFT** *Large grisaille panels of Joseph Dufour wallpaper illustrating Neoclassical scenes were brought from France two generations ago and installed in the living room.*

**RIGHT** *Beyond the gaming table is a comfortable library with coffered wood ceiling, low bookcases, and a gallery of family portraits.*

154

**LEFT AND BELOW FAR LEFT** *The small drawing room has been decorated with an array of 19th-century furniture in several styles. A large gilt 19th-century mirror covers the mantel wall. Family portraits are suspended from gold cords in an old-fashioned manner. An early 19th-century mahogany marqueterie pier table from the reign of Ferdinand VII is decorated with unusual chinoiserie motifs.*

**BELOW LEFT** *In the dining room, a reproduction of Velázquez's portrait of an infanta is set into a panel on the wall.*

RIGHT *On an Aubusson carpet in the dining room stand an English-style marqueterie table and caned-seat dining chairs.*

158

## OLD WORLD CHARM

Both in its architecture and interior decoration, the 17th-century house in the town of Pollensa exemplifies a typically Mallorcan esthetic. Belonging to the Llobera family — and now occupied by Miguel Llobera, a doctor whose practice is in Palma, Mallorca's capital — the mansion dominates Pollensa's Plaza Vieja.

All the rooms are organized around a wide double stair and furnished with a mix of antiques from different periods that mirrors the tastes of succeeding family generations.

**FAR LEFT AND LEFT** *Rocking chairs are lined up on the pebbled floor of the hall, a tradition in Mallorca.*

**CENTER LEFT AND BELOW CENTER LEFT** *Visitors to the house hang their canes on a special stand in the hall.*

**BELOW FAR LEFT** *The metal-studded leather Mallorcan chairs date from the 17th century. An 18th-century painting of Salome presenting the head of Saint John the Baptist is set off by an exuberantly carved gilded frame.*

**LEFT** *A plain bench is the only piece on the bedroom landing.*

**ABOVE RIGHT AND RIGHT** *Typically Mallorcan, an arch separates the entrance and stair hall. The monumental double staircase rises up for three floors.*

**ABOVE** *Small landscape paintings, fans, and decorative objects are randomly arranged in a tiny salon furnished with Alfonso XIII pieces. The brazier sits on a low table.*

**ABOVE** *The dining room is sparsely furnished. At mealtimes the balloon-back chairs are pulled up to the table.*

**ABOVE** *The geometric tiles in one of the bedrooms were probably installed during a 19th-century renovation.*

**ABOVE** *Family photographs are hung in the shape of a cross on a wall of the salon.*

**ABOVE** *Crammed with old books, the desk and bookcase occupy a corner of one of the bedrooms.*

**ABOVE** *The study on the ground floor belongs to the master of the house.*

**ABOVE**  *The traditional dish rack in the old kitchen allows water to drip back into the original huge stone sink.*

**LEFT**  *Ancient iron keys, no longer in use, now decorate the kitchen wall.*

**RIGHT**  *A "cool safe" hangs from the center of the shelf-lined pantry, protected from rodents and flying insects. A chorizo dries inside.*

## ARCHAEOLOGICAL SITE

Hacienda Micones, an olive grower's estate, is in the countryside outside Seville on the road to Cádiz. The sprawling Baroque house was built in 1749 by Tomás Micon, the first Marquis de Meritos.

Today, the estate belongs to Enrique Cortines and his wife, Loupe. His son, José, collected an unusual group of archaeological artifacts, as well as idiosyncratic furnishings. These elements give the handsome farm a sophisticated character.

**LEFT**  *A huge gate in the imposing facade leads to a central courtyard.*

**BELOW LEFT**  *Carefully clipped juniper topiary creates a formal garden.*

**ABOVE RIGHT**  *An arcade connects the entrance to the courtyard and outbuildings.*

**ABOVE CENTER RIGHT**  *The carved stone pillar protects the gate.*

**ABOVE FAR RIGHT**  *A classical Roman marble bust stands sentinel-like near the stairs that lead from the ground floor to the bedrooms.*

**RIGHT**  *As is customary in Andalusia, myriad plants in terra-cotta pots hang on window grilles and walls or stand on the ground.*

**CENTER RIGHT**  *A grove of date palms on one side of the house provides fruit.*

**FAR RIGHT**  *Tall curtained windows open directly onto the cobbled courtyard.*

**ABOVE** *The stair risers are decorated with traditional glazed tiles.*

**ABOVE** *Paintings, engravings, sculpture, and a grandfather clock decorate the stairwell.*

**ABOVE** *The formal dining room is used only for important receptions.*

**ABOVE** *Stag horns in the dining room are trophies from hunting parties of the past. A pair of early 18th-century carved wooden figures holding lanterns flanks the door.*

**ABOVE AND ABOVE RIGHT**  *Artifacts such as a polychromed statuette of the Infant Jesus protected by a glass dome, framed fans, and a mid–19th-century primitive portrait of an Andalusian girl coexist with a set of bamboo furniture that was made in the Philippines about 100 years ago.*

**LEFT, CENTER RIGHT, RIGHT AND FAR RIGHT**  *In the covered veranda on the ground floor are assembled the family's collection of ancient archaeological objects, including statuary and pottery.*

## PLEASANT PATIO

Situated in the Barrio de
Santa Cruz, the former
Jewish section of Seville, the
small house typifies the
elegance of the area with its
colorful ceramic tiles, flower-
filled patio, and decorative
wrought-iron grilles.

An American couple,
Campbell and Betty Engles,
has lived in the 18th-century
house since their retirement.
Originally there were two
kitchens in the house. In the
summer, one lived on the
cooler ground floor; in the
winter, on the floors above.
The only important change
the Campbells have made in
the house is to convert the
winter kitchen on the second
floor into a bedroom.

**ABOVE LEFT AND LEFT** *A multitude of hanging and potted plants fills the cool patio. The terra-cotta floor is inlaid with glazed tiles.*

**ABOVE** *The geometric design of the ceramic tiles is Moorish in influence. The Campbells restored the tilework with old tiles found in local antique shops.*

**RIGHT** *An elaborate wrought-iron grille leads from the narrow street onto the patio.*

**ABOVE AND RIGHT** *The dining room, on the ground floor, opens onto the street. The window is always kept open to take advantage of any breezes. The typically Sevillan openwork wooden screen near the window gives a measure of privacy.*

**FAR RIGHT** *The Campbells brought the pottery coffee set on the dining room table back from Tangier, a city in Morocco they visit often.*

**ABOVE** *On the second floor, a wide tiled-wall gallery encircles the courtyard.*

**FAR LEFT** *A flight of narrow tiled steps connects the second-floor gallery to the patio below.*

**LEFT** *Potted plants hanging over the courtyard can be glimpsed from the interior gallery windows.*

## ENGLISH STYLE

Mahón, the capital of the strategically placed island of Minorca, was under British rule throughout most of the 18th century. The English influence, particularly in architecture and furniture styles, has remained strong.

Antonia Vives Campomar, now in her late seventies, has lived in the small town house on the main street of Mahón since she was a young girl. Her house is filled with the mementos and heirlooms of a lifetime — family portraits and paintings, English antique furniture, and collections of china and knick-knacks.

**ABOVE** *A small mid–18th century shrine with a carved wood figure of the Infant Jesus occupies the top of a bureau in one of the bedrooms.*

**FAR LEFT AND CENTER LEFT**   *The narrow staircase, as in many Minorcan houses, is similar to those found in small English houses.*

**BELOW FAR LEFT**   *Family portraits and maritime scenes hang above the two Georgian-style side chairs that flank an 18th-century bench with a woven rush seat in the living room.*

**BELOW LEFT**   *Mid–19th century lusterware pitchers, porcelain figurines, and old glass are displayed in a Chippendale Revival secretary.*

**RIGHT**   *Family portraits in gilt or ebonized frames surround a 19th-century landscape above the console.*

**ABOVE**  *The living room with its English-influenced double-hung windows contains both 18th-century Georgian furniture and contemporary Spanish imitations in the English style. The uncarpeted marble floor is the strongest hint of the room's Spanish locale.*

**LEFT AND RIGHT**  *Naive paintings, many from the 19th century by Balearic Island artists, almost cover the living room walls.*

## FULL OF POETRY

Miguel Costa i Llobera, a famous Mallorcan poet, was born in 1854 in the small town of Pollensa on the rocky northern coast of the Island of Mallorca and died in Palma in 1922. His descendants now maintain the house, where the poet spent his entire life, in honor of his memory.

Like many other houses in the town, the low building is made of stone and is separated from the narrow street by an arched gateway. Very traditional in decor, the rooms bear witness to a disappearing era when formality and Old World customs were respected.

**ABOVE LEFT**  *At the bottom of the overgrown garden is a memorial bust of Miguel Costa i Llobera.*

**ABOVE FAR LEFT**  *A bridge suspended over the basement light well links the back of the house to the garden.*

**LEFT**  *The well stands beneath an ancient oleander at the bottom of the garden path.*

**ABOVE**  *An old stone and tiled sink near the basement functions as an outdoor extension to the kitchen.*

**RIGHT**  *The 19th-century religious painting in the hall reflects the poet's interest in mysticism.*

**ABOVE AND RIGHT** *The delicate early 19th-century brass and iron balustrade is the work of local craftsmen.*

**ABOVE** *In the main reception room, a suite of late Fernandino settees and chairs stands against the wall in the Mallorcan manner – a fashion that began in the 18th century.*

**LEFT** Azulejos *are inset into the terra-cotta tiled floor.*

**ABOVE**   *A pair of undulating sofas facing each other in the study exemplifies the exuberant Isabelino style of the mid-19th century.*

**RIGHT**   *A traditional feature of Mallorcan houses was a hinge system that permitted doors to be held open at an angle, preventing them from slamming shut in the wind.*

**FAR RIGHT**   *In the study, a glass-fronted cabinet holds the poet's papers, books, and memorabilia.*

**ABOVE**   *The old-fashioned family bedroom, with its overscale-patterned wallpaper, heavy draperies, matching upholstered chairs, and dark wood, recalls a time when midday heat required a quiet siesta.*

**LEFT**   *During the summer months, the hearth is covered with a fireboard depicting a Swiss chalet.*

# CHAPTER

# 7

# MODERN VIEWS

In the last decade, Spain has rediscovered not only a freedom of expression, but a desire for modernity. It has also reevaluated its recent cultural past.

Especially in Barcelona, a new generation of creative people — leaders in their fields — has taken charge of the movement. In the forefront are photographers, designers, and artists, who are expressing themselves in the places in which they live. While some look straight to the 21st century, others prefer to reflect on the masters of the Catalan *modernismo* — a 20th-century revolution that brought a period of unequaled virtuosity.

**ABOVE**   *Even the peephole on a door in a Barcelona building by Domenéch i Montaner has an ornamental quality.*

**RIGHT**   *The undulating roofline of glazed tiles is one of the most arresting features of Gaudí's 1906 Casa Battló on Barcelona's wide Passeig de Gracia.*

## WHIMSICAL TRIO

In Barcelona, in the residential area known as San Gervasio, Brigitte Szenczi, Juan Antonio Manas, and Vicenç Ferran share a large, conventional apartment that they have transformed into a surrealistic environment.

Szenczi and Manas are artists who work as a team to create bas reliefs, paintings, and sculptures. Along with Ferran, they own Dos i Una, a leading design shop in Barcelona.

The three have applied their skills to create a highly individualistic and whimsical scheme that is part theater, part studio, part home.

**LEFT** *The front door with its old-fashioned peephole opens onto the apartment building's modest stair hall.*

**LEFT** *One of the rooms of the apartment serves as a studio for Brigitte Szenczi and Juan Antonio Manas. The painting on the easel is one of their collaborations.*

**RIGHT** *The artists have added their own wooden arrows to a mammoth papier-mâché head of a sailor made for a carnival to create a playful composition atop the bookcase.*

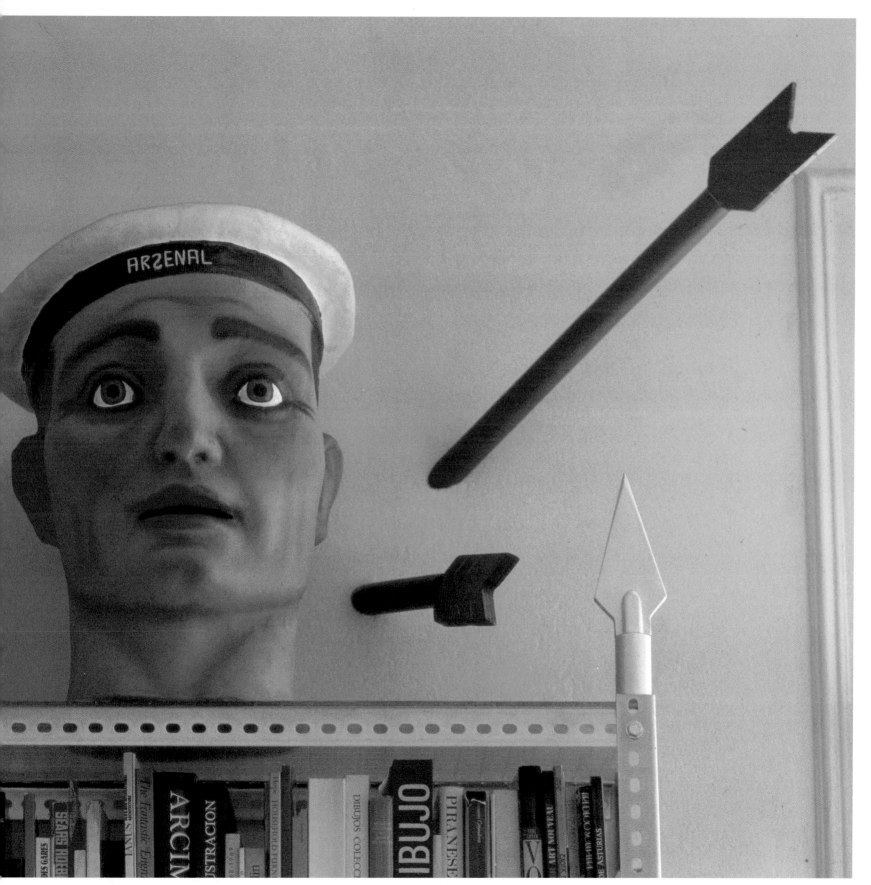

**ABOVE** *In the hallway, a niche painted with a backdrop of sky and sea sets off a three-dimensional aquatic collage that includes a plaster Ionic column, a 1950s octopus candelabrum, and two plastic fish.*

**LEFT** *With a papier-mâché shell for a base and branches of painted coral holding the lights, a fantasy lamp continues the seaside theme in the dining room.*

**ABOVE RIGHT AND ABOVE FAR RIGHT** *Painted ceilings and walls, trompe l'oeil niches, and sculptured accessories in the dining room add to the apartment's surrealistic look.*

**RIGHT** *In contrast to the other rooms, the kitchen is sleek and modern, with a central work counter and sinuous stove hood. Plastic lilies add a stylish touch.*

**FAR RIGHT** *A long hallway connects the rooms of the apartment.*

RIGHT *In Brigitte Szenczi's bedroom, a chest has been painted in grisaille. The mirror, picture frames, and cupid-based lamp with its tulle shade are in the same neutral hue.*

**ABOVE**  In a corner of the living room are two of the artists' surrealistic works made from found objects.

**RIGHT**  Sweeping red draperies add drama to the otherwise white-on-white living room with its classical references. All the furniture is draped in white cotton canvas. Sheer curtains diffuse the light from the ample bay window.

**ABOVE** *The Ionic column outside the dining room window inspired the classical imagery within. The 1950s glass fish came from the Barcelona flea market.*

## ARTIST'S VILLAGE

Many years ago, Xavier Corberó, a modern sculptor, fell under the charm of Esplugas, a village on the outskirts of Barcelona. He bought a small house there — mainly to save it from demolition — and gradually turned it into a home for himself and his wife, Maria Luisa Tiffon, a psychiatrist.

Outbuildings — a guest house and studios for visiting artists — came next; later, a 17th-century house complete with 19th-century wall paintings was turned into a private museum.

While he has added some modern features, such as a swimming pool, Corberó has retained the essential characteristics that first attracted him to the house. The furnishings and materials are simple, and the objects — collected over years — are personal and evocative.

**LEFT** *A bromeliad hangs on the well-worn heavy front door of the house.*

**RIGHT** *The lush garden, with its swimming pool and columned patio, acts as a connection between the buildings in the complex. The iron gates and ancient stone wash trough are now the entrance and fountain for the guest house.*

**ABOVE**  *The 17th-century house on the hill is now a museum and storage space for some of the sculptor's contemporary pieces.*

**FAR LEFT, LEFT, AND BELOW LEFT**  *The wooden beams and plaster walls were painted in the 19th century. Formal dinners are sometimes served in the romantic rooms.*

**FAR LEFT**  *California Roll is the name of the six-foot-high marble, pyrite, and granite 1986 work by Corberó.*

ABOVE   *Xavier Corberó sits in the garden behind one of the small village houses he has renovated.*

RIGHT   *Gavina, a 1980 sculpture (far right) and* Corberebus, *from the late 1970s, are two of the pieces displayed in the museum.*

ABOVE  *A player piano stands in the foyer of one of the village houses that has been renovated for guests and visiting artists. The piano was traditionally played for* manubrios – *street festivals.*

LEFT  *A collection of* dolorosas – *19th-century wood Madonna mannequins – peers from a high ledge in the bedroom.*

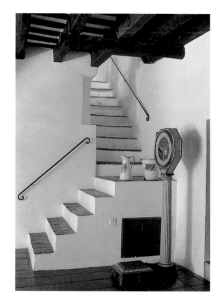

ABOVE    *An antique scale that once belonged to Juan Manuel Serrat, a folksinger, stands by the stone stair in the guest house. Iron handrails are set into the walls.*

RIGHT    *The 19th-century iron bed is typically Catalan. The washstand is original to the interior.*

RIGHT    *On the ground floor, an 18th-century grandfather clock stands near an antique pool table.*

**ABOVE** *The white walls in the guest house kitchen contrast with the dark Spanish table and chairs from Aragon. Jugs and bottles parade along a high shelf. The* porrón, or carafe, *on the table is traditional for drinking wine.*

**ABOVE** *Simple wood folding chairs and a gate-leg table furnish the kitchen.*

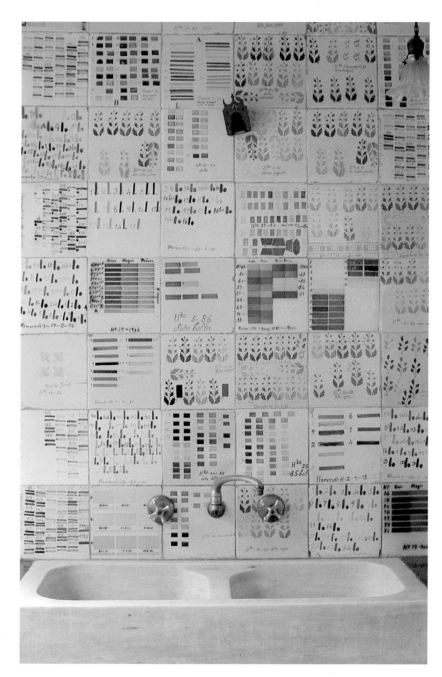

**ABOVE** *Mismatched tiles, vintage samples bought inexpensively from a local pottery, create an intriguing quiltlike pattern. The warm colors were created with vegetable dyes.*

**ABOVE** *In the glass-fronted kitchen cabinet, the sculptor has assembled a collection of colorful kitsch and folk art objects – including water bottles in the shape of matadors and infantas.*

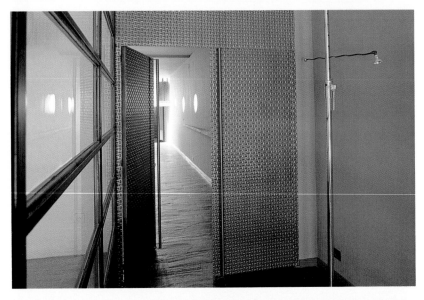

## VERTICAL LOFT

In Barcelona, a city on the cutting edge of design, many of the new generation of designers are sensitive to a changing lifestyle and are adapting their living and working environments to suit their needs. One of the most radical is Lluís Moron, a graphic designer.

His unusual loft is in a small building with a roof terrace. The interior was completely gutted to create three open spaces. The renovation project is a collaboration between Moron, Vicenç Viaplana, an artist, and Amadeu Clusella, an architect. Most surprising is the placement of the swimming pool just inside the entrance.

**ABOVE LEFT, LEFT, AND BELOW LEFT** *A long narrow corridor dotted with lights in the shape of portholes leads from the front door down several steps to the indoor swimming pool.*

**RIGHT** *Lluís Moron (far right) and Amadeu Clusella, the architect with whom he worked on the renovation, sit around the kitchen table.*

**FAR LEFT** *Vicenç Viaplana, a Spanish artist, painted the bottom of the pool.*

**LEFT AND BELOW LEFT** *The kitchen is open to the dining room. The large table, surrounded with Café Costes chairs by Philippe Starck, often serves as a conference table for business meetings. The natural light comes from a greenhouse enclosure on the floor above.*

**CENTER FAR LEFT AND BELOW FAR LEFT** *Near the swimming pool, mirrored panels separate the toilet and shower from the double sink unit in the open bathroom.*

**BELOW LEFT** *The pool room on the second floor is illuminated by a skylight by day. The wall's murals are by Vicenç Viaplana.*

**RIGHT** *A Ya Ya Ho lamp by Ingo Maurer, the German designer, provides spotlighting under the stars at night.*

## YOUTHFUL APPROACH

Ines and Ramon Parellada and their small son live on the *principal* — the floor reserved for the building's original owner — in an apartment house built by a student of Puig i Cadalfalch, one of the most famous architects of the Catalan modernist movement.

The building is situated in the center of Barcelona, near the Passeig de Gracia, one of the city's main avenues. When the young couple moved into the huge apartment, they decided not to be overpowered by its formality and instead to give it the flavor of their own freewheeling way of life. So far, the Parelladas — he owns a fashionable restaurant in the Barri Gótic, she is a painter — occupy only the rear rooms of the apartment, which face the garden and were meant to be used primarily in summer. The darker rooms, which face the street and were once the grand reception rooms, are used as a painting studio.

**FAR LEFT** *The building's large lobby boasts a double staircase and a vintage elevator, the first in Barcelona.*

**LEFT** *Many of the windows of the* principal *floor apartment overlook the street.*

**ABOVE** *The elevator shaft is in an inner courtyard. The still-working elevator was built by Josep Maria Jujol, a student and disciple of Antonio Gaudí.*

**FAR LEFT** *The front door opens onto a foyer with a floor of colorful tiles.*

**CENTER LEFT AND BELOW CENTER LEFT** *Most of the doors have glass panels etched with delicate floral designs.*

**LEFT** *The inlaid parquet floors and ceilings ringed with gilded moldings recall the former grandeur and lavish decor of one of the front reception rooms.*

**BELOW FAR LEFT** *A hallway follows the contour of the central courtyard around the apartment, and is lined with windows in a geometric pattern. The light on the floor is a neon tube with a paper shade devised by Ramon Parellada. A Japanese paper lantern by Isamu Noguchi is similar in spirit.*

**LEFT** *Throw pillows covered in fabric by Mariscal, a young Catalan artist and designer, are the only elements of color in the rather plain bedroom.*

**ABOVE RIGHT** *The kitchen has been completely renovated. Only the cement tile floor was preserved.*

**RIGHT** *The dining room combines high-tech hanging lamps with wicker furniture and Scandinavian lighting. A pass-through provides easy access to the kitchen.*

211

**RIGHT AND BELOW** *A wide veranda stretches the whole width of the apartment at the rear above the garden. The furniture is by the Finnish architect Alvar Aalto, the hanging lamp by Ingo Maurer.*

**LEFT AND BELOW** *The living room, next to the veranda, is furnished with contemporary pieces. The overscale upholstered pieces are Italian, the 1940s-style lamps are by Santa & Cole, a Catalan company.*

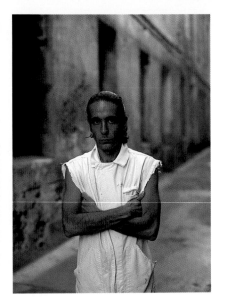

## ON THE MEZZANINE

A young artist professionally known as Tito lives and works in a former sugar factory in an industrial area in Barcelona. A sculptor, Tito works exclusively with human hair recycled from hairdressers, washing it, compacting it, and sculpting it into monoliths. Keeping the loft space open, Tito has confined his living quarters to the mezzanine.

The artist has designed everything in his environment — from the painted carpeting on the floor to the bizarre furniture that includes an aquarium-like coffee table and a bathtub on wheels.

**ABOVE LEFT**  *Tito's studio stands on a dead end street.*

**FAR LEFT**  *The artist drives a jeep. The body has been covered with real fur, in keeping with his preoccupation with hair.*

**ABOVE**  *All of Tito's creations have an element of surprise. The thronelike chair rolls on three wheels; the coffee table suspends a rock collection in Plexiglas.*

**RIGHT**  *The painted bathtub has been set up on a luggage rack on wheels and is left out in the open.*

216

**ABOVE** *An empty frame hangs above a sofa casually draped with cashmere paisley shawls.*

**RIGHT** *Winged putti painted on the trompe l'oeil Rococo-style ceiling recall the splendor of the past.*

**ABOVE**  *A modern painting hangs above a carved dark wood neo-Gothic cabinet. Under the glass are brides' headdresses of shell flowers that used to be made by women in Mallorca.*

**LEFT**  *In the smaller sitting room, a Victorian chandelier is suspended from the molding-laden ceiling.*

**FAR LEFT AND LEFT** *Small works of art, vintage photographs, and an antique mirror seem always to have hung on the damask-covered walls.*

**CENTER LEFT** *The floral tracery on the transom window and the door panel in the narrow back hall near the kitchen is sandblasted.*

**BELOW FAR LEFT** *In the dining room, painted panels with iris, bamboo, and bird motifs reflect the late 19th-century fascination with Japan and its art.*

**BELOW CENTER LEFT** *The patterns of the cement tile floor coordinate with the painted frieze on the baseboard in the dining room.*

**BELOW LEFT** *An antique lace spread covers the bed in a sleeping alcove.*

**RIGHT** *In the old days, the wooden articulated mannequin, a Madonna, would have been clothed.*

## PLAIN AND SIMPLE

Blai Puig, the artistic director of Pilma, a home furnishings company, lives in Barcelona in an apartment building that dates from the end of the 19th century.

The monochromatic color scheme — everything is white or pale in hue — gives a cool, atmospheric, and updated look to the classically laid-out space. The signs of the interior's architectural past include stucco moldings, arched French doors, sand-blasted glass, and stained-glass windows. These antique elements, heightened by the simple treatment of walls and woodwork, balance the contemporary look with charm and nostalgia.

**RIGHT**   *A brass peephole is set like a jewel on the black-lacquered front door.*

**BELOW**   *The dining room is simply and elegantly furnished with a set of early 20th-century chairs. The seats are slipcovered in white cotton.*

**LEFT** *The sandblasted glass windows and doors as well as the glass-filled arch are characteristic of apartments of the era.*

**BELOW** *While the look of the all-white kitchen is contemporary, only old-fashioned materials, such as marble and ceramic tile, have been used. White cotton curtains close off the below-the-counter shelves.*

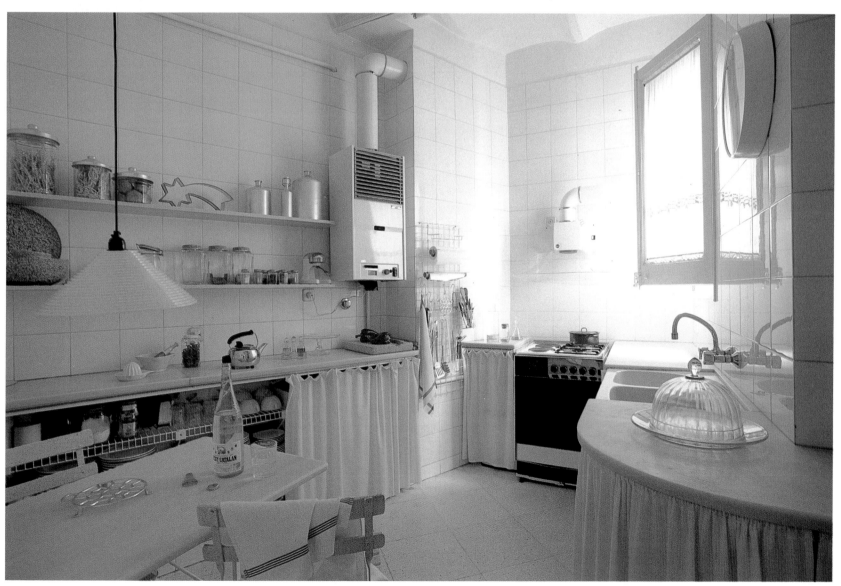

**ABOVE** *An ornate stained-glass window is reflected in the glossy, flagstone floor.*

**ABOVE** *A French door opens onto a small study.*

**ABOVE** *The master bedroom is dominated by an antique carved and mirrored armoire.*

**ABOVE** *The old-fashioned sink and lace-trimmed shower curtain soften the look of the immaculate all-white bathroom.*

# CHAPTER

# 8

# ON VACATION

In Spain — in spite of the 50 million tourists who go there every year, and who have so irrevocably changed the coast and island resorts — there are still many places that have remained oases of serenity.

The pleasure of having a house that one can retreat to, not only for the long summer vacation but on weekends and for short visits during the year, is inestimable. Vacation homes — whether those that have welcomed generations of a family on annual visits, or simple dwellings for a refreshingly rudimentary way of life, or gracious, well-appointed houses where sophisticated entertaining is a relaxation — are the places for the times of the year when the only person to please is oneself.

**ABOVE** *A woven straw shade is pulled down against the heat of the day during siesta time in Andalusia.*

**RIGHT** *Olive trees dot the rolling Andalusian hills.*

## VILLAGE HOUSE

Minorca, the second largest of the Balearic Islands after Mallorca, is still relatively unspoiled and not overly developed. José Luis Gil de la Galleja and Aurora Poveda Amadon, owners of Agua de Limon, a well-known modern design shop in Valencia, have renovated a modest house in the inland village of Alayor, in the north of the island.

Set directly on the street, the house has a traditional whitewashed facade; an unexpected garden flourishes in the rear. The couple have respected the original layout of the house. The small rooms are minimally but charmingly furnished with their flea market finds and collections of folk art objects.

**ABOVE**  *The austere facade is punctuated with a double-hung shuttered window, one of the signs of the English influence on the island.*

**FAR LEFT** *In the rear garden, a well provides fresh water. The deep sink was originally used for laundry.*

**ABOVE** *Ceramic parakeets perch on stands set into the stone wall.*

**LEFT AND RIGHT** *An iron table and metal folding chairs have been set up on the tiled terrace under the shade of the grape arbor.*

**LEFT**   *A collection of holy water fonts, religious images, and a series of silver ex-votos hang as decoration in the entrance hall.*

**BELOW LEFT AND BELOW RIGHT**   *The small ground-floor sitting room, with its rustic painted furniture, sometimes doubles as a guest room.*

**RIGHT, CENTER RIGHT, AND BELOW FAR RIGHT**   *The centrally placed staircase with lacquered banister is influenced by English architectural styles.*

**FAR RIGHT**   *The entrance hall also serves as a small study. A woven straw carpet covers the diamond-patterned tiled floor.*

**BELOW CENTER RIGHT**   *Antique puppets are crowded in a built-in cupboard that closes with an Art Nouveau–style carved wood and glass door.*

**ABOVE** *In one of the bedrooms, an early 20th-century washstand has been painted dark green, a popular color in Minorca.*

**LEFT** *A 19th-century bench with a rush seat is an example of traditional Balearic furniture.*

**ABOVE**  *The appeal of the master bedroom lies in its unpretentious and eclectic mix of late 19th-century furnishings.*

**LEFT**  *The many ledges in the house serve to show off collections. Clear glass candlesticks rest on a ledge in one of the bathrooms.*

**ABOVE** *The woodwork in the spacious kitchen with its vaulted ceiling has been painted in an unusual shade of bright pink.*

**RIGHT** *Dried herbs in pottery jars stand on top of the refrigerator.*

**ABOVE**  *A window separates the kitchen from the interior dining room. Two bentwood settees replace chairs as seating at either end of the table. A hand-painted frieze encircles the beamed-ceilinged room.*

**LEFT**  *A ceramic figurine sits on the wide ledge of the kitchen window.*

## GRAND SCHEME

Paco Muñoz, one of Spain's most famous interior decorators, was one of the first to discover the romantic charms of Pedraza, a medieval town imbued with a chivalric past.

Years ago, he started the renovation of a group of village houses, restructuring them into a series of connected spacious rooms. With his wife, Sabine Deroulede, Muñoz spends nearly every weekend in Pedraza. His influence is far-reaching. In one of the village's grand houses he has established De Natura, a home furnishings shop known for its antiques, crafts objects, and contemporary folk art furniture.

In his own home, Muñoz has displayed his interior design signature—the bold mix of overscale traditional Spanish furnishings with contemporary artworks.

**LEFT, BELOW LEFT AND BELOW RIGHT** *On a clear day the formal garden behind the house offers a panoramic view of the countryside around Pedraza, a village perched on a hill.*

**RIGHT** *A cobbled terrace is an extension of the dining room. Rustic chairs and a country table create a relaxed, informal setting under a pergola.*

**TOP**   The house with its 16th-century facade stands behind an arcade off the Plaza Mayor.

**ABOVE**   A bowling game from the Basque region is one of the folk art objects Paco Muñoz appreciates for its form and craftsmanship.

**RIGHT**   Inside the front door, the majestic foyer features a pebbled floor and a pair of oversize antique curved benches that came from a chapel choir.

**ABOVE** *Carved objects of different shapes in one of the living rooms offer a variety of textures.*

**RIGHT** *Creating a high-ceilinged living room with a wide bay window was one of the goals of the renovation.*

**ABOVE** *The painted antique cabinet once belonged to an herbalist who stocked the medicinal herbs illustrated on the drawers.*

**LEFT** *White cotton fabric dresses sofa, chairs, and even the coffee table in one of the sitting rooms.*

**FAR LEFT** *Overlooking the garden is a small flower-arranging room suitably decorated with an old herbal on a reading stand and framed botanical prints.*

**LEFT** *The wide mezzanine over the living room functions as a library.*

**BELOW CENTER FAR LEFT** *A painting by Lucio Muñoz, a Spanish artist, hangs above a medieval Spanish console.*

**BELOW CENTER LEFT** *A sculpture by Eduardo Chillida is the focus of the glass-windowed space on the half-mezzanine.*

**BELOW FAR LEFT AND BELOW LEFT** *Contemporary paintings by Spanish artists, including a large work by Antoni Tápies, hang in the two basement sitting rooms.*

**RIGHT** *A collection of idiosyncratic objects, including an antique globe, a woodworker's masterpiece of a church model, a classical marble statue, and an ancient leather-bound manuscript bear witness to Paco Muñoz's eclectic taste and interests.*

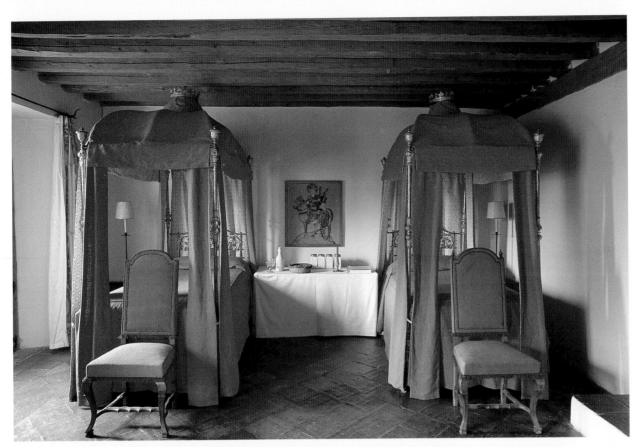

**LEFT** *Gilded crowns top the pair of coral-hued fabric-draped canopy beds in one of the guest rooms.*

**BELOW LEFT** *Two 19th-century painted iron beds with floral motifs furnish a guest room.*

RIGHT *One of the children's rooms includes an extraordinary iron-and-brass convent bed that was used only on the night a nun took her vows.*

BELOW RIGHT *An unusual marqueterie bed in a traditional Mallorcan shape is the center of attention in another bedroom.*

## RESTFUL REFUGE

Since 1965, the American artist Elaine Lustig Cohen has been spending part of each summer on the island of Mallorca. She discovered the house in which she lives by accident.

Set in a remote village far from the bustle of tourists, the whitewashed stone house has always been considered by its owner as a magic restorative place where she can savor isolation without the burden of loneliness. Cohen, who is also a dealer of 20th-century art books, posters, ephemera, and catalogues, has filled the multilevel house with her own artworks as well as mementos from travels all over the world.

**ABOVE LEFT** *A wrought-iron gate gives the house an added sense of privacy.*

**FAR LEFT** *Wine is often enjoyed at a stone table on the terrace.*

**LEFT** *Three Mallorcan chairs are set out on a terrace that offers a panoramic view of the surrounding countryside.*

**ABOVE** *Bright sunlight creates a pattern on the whitewashed wall.*

**RIGHT** *The surprisingly sophisticated Austrian chairs, bought from a gypsy on the island, are an audacious contrast to the rustic whitewashed fireplace.*

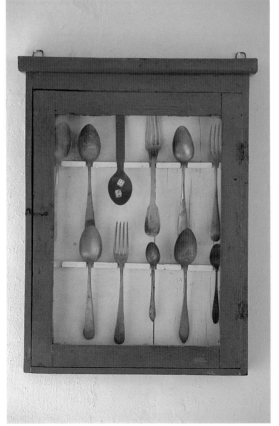

**ABOVE FAR LEFT**  The interior is made up of a series of volumes fashioned out of stone. The sofas are simple banquettes topped wth pillows.

**ABOVE LEFT**  The library and dining room are at the end of a corridor that stretches above the living room. An iron stove, imported from Scandinavia, heats the house off-season.

**ABOVE**  A double niche holds a Mexican folk art horse and china bought on Mallorca. A thick whitewashed stone banister rings the stair that leads to the bedrooms.

**FAR LEFT**  The portrait of the French poet Arthur Rimbaud is part of the Illuminations by Sonia Delaunay, the Constructivist painter.

**LEFT**  The spoon holder has become a conceptual artwork of found objects by Elaine Lustig Cohen.

**RIGHT** *An African bird, two Mexican crosses, and a carved wood angel, as well as one of the artist's collages, are arranged on and around a Guatemalan table.*

**BELOW RIGHT** *The 1897 poster depicting a bull was a gift from a gypsy to Elaine Lustig Cohen's late husband.*

251

## ON THE SQUARE

Agnes and Alejandro Masso — she works in an interior design firm in Madrid, he is a composer — spend long weekends and vacation time in Pedraza, near Segovia. Their 16th-century house is on the Plaza Mayor, the main square of the picturesque medieval village.

The rustic house is one of a group of structures framed with porticoes that are topped with heraldic coats of arms carved in stone and covered with deep loggias. Inside, the spacious rooms have been furnished with a combination of fine Spanish antiques and 19th-century folk art pieces.

**ABOVE LEFT AND LEFT**  *Spacious entrance halls function as living rooms. The well-worn terra-cotta floors have been waxed for centuries.*

**LEFT** *Originally two houses, the Massos' residence has two front doors, which open directly onto Pedraza's historic Plaza Mayor.*

**RIGHT** *In one of the halls, a turned gateleg table holds a polychromed shrine.*

**ABOVE**　*A small cell-like bedroom is adjacent to the foyer.*

**ABOVE LEFT**　*In the back of the house, logs are piled up ready to be used for outdoor cooking on the ancient stove.*

**LEFT**　*A small roofed terrace overlooks the back garden.*

**ABOVE**   A carved wood shelf decorated with shells and dried flowers serves as a double candle holder in the dining room.

**ABOVE RIGHT**   In the dining room, the long refectory table is flanked with benches; a pair of high-backed rush chairs sit at head and foot. Another bench, with a scalloped back, separates the dining room from the kitchen.

**RIGHT**   The redesigned fireplace in the second-floor sitting room is one of the few contemporary touches in the house. The easy chairs are slipcovered in white cotton for the summer.

**LEFT AND ABOVE**   *The 19th-century folk art settee, chairs, and chest on the loggia were bought from gypsies in Andalusia. Originally painted, they are now stripped and bleached. White-glazed terra-cotta ornaments frequently decorate Andalusian rooftops.*

## PIONEERING SPIRIT

A few years ago, Patrick and Fanny Dupin decided to turn their vacation lifestyle into a permanent one. Leaving jobs in Paris behind, the French couple settled on the island of Ibiza. They now live in a small farmhouse, or finca, called Can Llatxe (Saint Lazarus), in the countryside near the village of Jesus.

The Dupins' life revolves around such activities as fishing, gardening, reading, boating, and swimming. Much of their time is spent renovating their house, using their own hands to augment limited financial means.

**ABOVE**   *The rounded oven, seen from the back, is typically found in many fincas on Ibiza.*

**LEFT**   *At dusk, the house is lit with many candles and kerosene lamps. The pleasure of dining by candlelight more than compensates for the lack of electricity.*

**RIGHT**   *A rustic wooden gate leads to a cobbled foyer.*

**ABOVE** *The house still has its primitive roof, constructed in layers – thick beams overlaid with branches that support a thick layer of earth.*

**RIGHT** *The delicate antique French portrait of a woman in a classical pose contrasts with the thick white beamed ceiling and the heavy dark wood door. Leaving the canvas unframed has allowed it to blend in with the surroundings.*

**ABOVE** *Ceramics and glass are displayed in a small cabinet set into the wall.*

**LEFT** *Although new, the bathroom has been given a rustic look. Unusually located in that it is open to the main living area, it includes a deep stone tub.*

**LEFT** *The combination dining and living room has been accommodated in what was originally the house's kitchen. The huge chimney covers the whole room.*

**ABOVE** *The rooms are furnished modestly, as they would have been in the past. The carved wooden chest serves as storage.*

**ABOVE AND RIGHT**
*Although the Louis XV–style piano may seem odd in a rustic kitchen, it gives warmth and a dash of eccentricity to the plain surroundings, where music plays an important part.*

## BY THE SEA

Along the Mediterranean near Sitges, on Spain's eastern coast, are basic wooden boathouses under which fishermen stored their boats and sometimes spent the night. These boathouses are now sought after by a new generation of vacationers who eschew the traditional trappings of luxury. One of these huts belongs to a Catalan businessman who uses it as a weekend escape from his hectic city life.

**TOP** *In the boating tradition, many of the cottages bear women's names. "Lola" is the new name that was given to one of the wooden huts.*

**ABOVE** *Javier Mariscal, a Catalan artist, spent the weekend in Sitges and stenciled a vignette of a fisherman.*

**ABOVE LEFT, LEFT, AND RIGHT**   *The simple huts on pilings were built directly on the sandy beach.*

**ABOVE**   *The tiny interior is one multifunctional room.*

## FORMER FARMHOUSE

Since World War II, Palma de Mallorca has become an important European tourist center. Most inhabitants of the Island of Mallorca live in Palma, the capital and largest city, but many others maintain vacation homes elsewhere on the 1,400-square-mile island.

Miguel Servera Blanes, the director of the Fundació Pilar i Joan Miró, spends the summer months in Campanet on an established estate near the center of the island. For previous owners the land's bounty of figs, olives, and game was a source of revenue.

For the last 10 years, Blanes has gradually been restoring the farmhouse. Because of his taste for contemporary art, his efforts are less directed to historic preservation than to the creation of an eclectic interior in which objects and furnishings from different periods comfortably coexist.

**ABOVE RIGHT** *The view from the house looks across the dramatic landscape at the center of the island.*

**RIGHT** *Behind the house is an ambitious vegetable garden with plants set in diagonal rows.*

266

**ABOVE** *The arched doorway of the stone farmhouse is traditionally Mallorcan, and an elegant contrast with the stark facade.*

**LEFT** *Four matching rocking chairs complement the cobbled paving of the front courtyard.*

**ABOVE** *Inside the front entrance, a gracious arch that dates from the 13th century separates the large foyer from the adjacent hall, a typical layout for Mallorcan houses. The hook at the center of the arch once held a scale for weighing farm produce offered for sale to visiting merchants.*

**LEFT** *A row of 17th-century metal-studded chairs with leather seats and backs from Mallorca and a long sofa furnish the foyer. The open staircase is in the Gothic Mallorcan style.*

**ABOVE** *The small sitting room is focused around the stone fireplace, above which hangs a painting by Robert Llimos, a contemporary Spanish artist.*

**LEFT** *Josep Guinovart painted the niche in the living room. The pottery is made on the islands.*

269

**ABOVE AND RIGHT** *In an arrangement typical of the island, the dining table is in the center of the room and the chairs are lined up against the wall between meals. A brasero, or brazier, stands underneath the table for warmth, and lemons grown on the property fill compotes.*

**BELOW LEFT AND BELOW** *The kitchen stove, stone sinks, and dish drying rack recall domestic activities of the past.*

**TOP**   *A small antechamber links a bathroom to one of the bedrooms.*

**ABOVE**   *A Mallorcan four-poster bed is draped in cotton.*

**ABOVE**   *An iron bed is half-hidden behind a lace curtain in a ground-floor alcove.*

**ABOVE AND ABOVE RIGHT**   *In the attic, under the eaves, Felix de Cardenas, a contemporary Spanish artist, has created a fanciful bucolic wall mural.*

## ROUGHING IT

Maria Josefa and Federico Hilario, a fashionable young couple who own a modern home furnishings design shop in Tarragona, spend their summer vacation in a tiny former sheep pen.

Situated in the rugged countryside near the village of San Luis in the south of the Island of Minorca, the stone structure is virtually empty. There is no plumbing or electricity, and cooking, bathing, and relaxing all take place outdoors. Inside, the bed is a mattress on the floor.

This simple lifestyle nevertheless reflects a sophisticated point of view — the need to be as one with nature, if only for a couple of months a year.

**ABOVE** *The angled walls have been constructed with stones set without mortar.*

**ABOVE FAR LEFT AND LEFT**
*A small cistern on the roof is filled with water from the well. A long hose and an enameled tin basin are the only fixtures in this roofless bathroom. The terra-cotta tiled roof has been whitewashed as is traditional on the island.*

**ABOVE** *A single tiny window is the sheep pen's only improvement.*

**TOP RIGHT** *A roughly crafted wooden gate marks the path near the house.*

**CENTER RIGHT** *A separate tiny building sometimes doubles as a guest room.*

**RIGHT** *An old table found in the village furnishes the outdoor "dining room."*

**RIGHT**  *Lemonade is a favorite beverage in Minorca, where lemons are plentiful. A butane gas refrigerator provides ice cubes.*

**BELOW RIGHT**  *The outdoor kitchen includes a tiled and whitewashed stone counter and a butane gas stove.*

**LEFT** *Rough-hewn pottery crafted on the island is used both for cooking and for serving the simple meals that are prepared outdoors. Basil is grown in a pot and is used to flavor many dishes.*

## INFORMAL ENTERTAINMENT

Ibiza — with its flat-roofed, all whitewashed houses (which have earned it the nickname the White Island) — resembles the Greek Islands more than it does its sister Balearics. In the last two decades it has become a favorite resort for foreigners who wish to vacation informally yet stylishly.

Twenty years ago, Catherine Garrelet, a Frenchwoman, fell in love with a finca in that part of the island called Las Salinas, or The Saltpans. Over the years, pieces and objects brought from France have joined the locally discovered furnishings.

The large combination kitchen and dining room is the most convivial part of the house, and therefore the most important for a house devoted to entertaining friends.

**ABOVE**  *Olive and fig trees grow in the countryside around the finca.*

**LEFT**  *Two cats laze on a sofa during the afternoon siesta.*

**TOP RIGHT**  *The house boasts a view over Las Salinas, 160 acres of salt marsh still used as a source of salt.*

**ABOVE RIGHT AND RIGHT**  *The covered terrace, extending from the living room, is typical of the finca.*

**ABOVE**   In the summer, a cashmere shawl camouflages the stove in the living room. A Moorish brazier is used as a low coffee table.

**LEFT**   A pair of Rococo-style easy chairs, upholstered in red velvet, contrasts with the rustic look of the farmhouse.

ABOVE, RIGHT, AND FAR
RIGHT  *The monumental
fireplace with huge chimney,
nearly encompassing the
whole kitchen, is a traditional
architectural element of the
finca. Herbs hang to dry from
benches on the ceiling. Ibiza
pottery, used for cooking, is
stored on the mantel shelf.*

## MONASTIC ABODE

A stone windmill and its outbuildings comprise an unusual summer retreat on the Island of Ibiza. Instead of renovating the structures, the occupant decided to leave the whitewashed house just as it always had been.

Behind high walls, geraniums bloom in profusion in the courtyard. Inside, a few pieces of locally crafted furniture provide the bare necessities in the nearly monastic interior.

**FAR LEFT**   *Tall double doors open onto the main courtyard.*

**LEFT**   *A green door closes off the well outside the property.*

**FAR LEFT**   *The iron door knocker has announced the arrival of visitors for generations.*

**LEFT**   *The door of one of the small outbuildings has been roughly outlined in whitewash.*

**BELOW FAR LEFT**   *Tomatoes dry in a barn near the house.*

**BELOW LEFT**   *A grape arbor shades the courtyard. The stone disks were originally part of the olive-oil presses.*

**RIGHT**   *The walls of the windmill are made of stones and a traditional cement of earth and lime.*

**ABOVE** All the rooms open onto a main living space. The stone floor is partly covered with rush mats made locally.

**LEFT AND RIGHT** Soot has blackened the stone part of the kitchen walls, which are plastered below with a mixture of earth and lime. A piece of newspaper, used in a primitive fashion, is meant to protect the wall.

286

**JAMONES**

**CASA ESPECIAL EN JAMONES Y EMBUTIDOS**

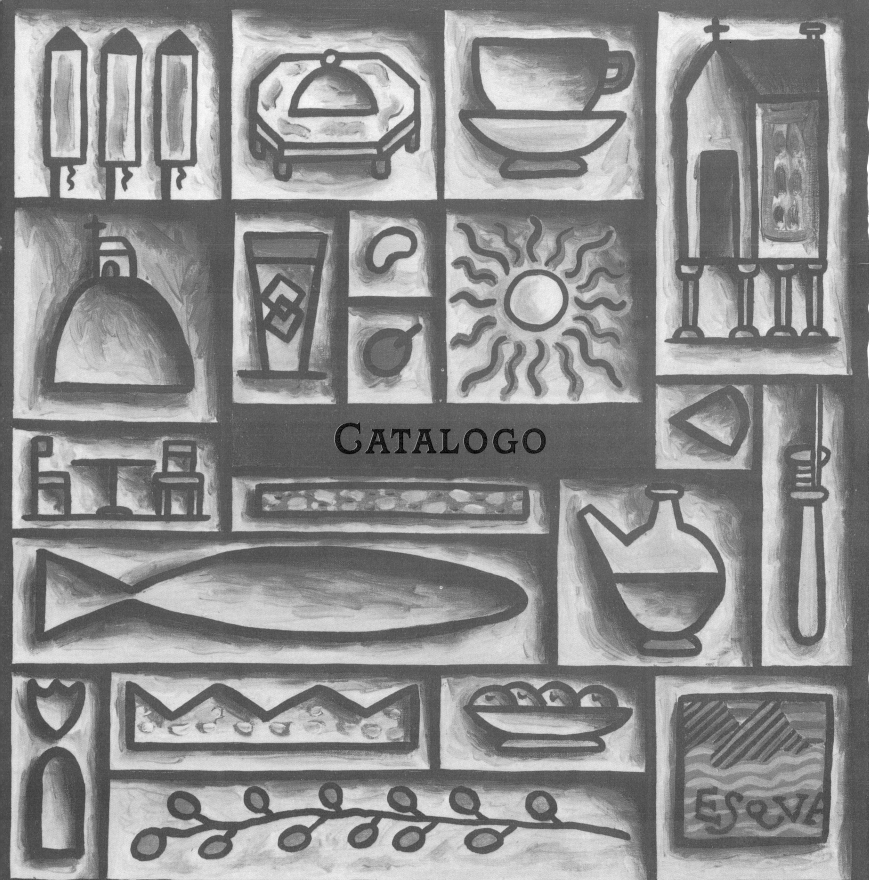

CATALOGO

# ARCHITECTURE AND DESIGN

## ARCON
Wooden chest with high-relief carving, often used for dowries.

## AZULEJOS
Glazed ceramic tiles with geometric motifs, used on both interior and exterior walls. They probably first appeared in Seville sometime in the 12th century.

## BODEGA
Wine cellar where barrels are kept and aged.

## BRASERO
Metal charcoal brazier, placed under the table and used for warmth.

## CALDERA
Covered wood-and-brass container traditionally used to carry water.

## CHIRINGUITO
Small, beachside wooden stand ranging from a primitive bar offering refreshments to a more substantial restaurant where paella is prepared and served.

## CHURRIGUERESQUE
The sumptuous and exaggerated Baroque style of the 18th century, named after the Churriguera family of architects.

## CORTIJO OR HACIENDA
Ranch or farm, typical of Andalusia, in the south.

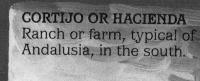

## CRUCERO
Stone roadside cross, often ornately carved. A series marked the pilgrimage route to Santiago de Compostela.

## ESCUDO DE ARMAS
Heraldic coat of arms carved in stone over doorways of buildings inhabited by those of noble lineage.

## FAROLA
Ubiquitous ironwork lantern.

## FRAILERO
Friar's chair, typically Spanish armchair from the early 17th to the mid-18th century, based on an Italian design.

## GALERIA
A distinctive glass-enclosed gallery designed to trap light and heat, common in the north.

## HORREO
Stone agricultural storage barn or granary, typical of the northern Atlantic coastal areas.

## MIRADOR
Glass-enclosed overhanging balcony, often commanding a view of a plaza or street.

## MODERNISMO
Architectural style of the Catalan renaissance that reinterpreted Gothic, Islamic, and Renaissance styles to form a "modernist" esthetic with parallels to Art Nouveau.

## MUDEJAR
Muslim decorative and architectural work executed under Christian rule during the 11th through 15th centuries.

## MUEBLES FERNANDINO
Furniture from the time of King Ferdinand VII (1808-1833), an opulent style that features carved wood swans and eagles.

## MUEBLES ISABELINO
Furniture from the time of Queen Isabella II (1833-1868), a romantic style roughly equivalent to the English Victorian.

## PATIO
A square courtyard in a house, surrounded by rooms on all sides. The most elaborate may include gardens and a central fountain. Typical of southern Spain with its Mediterranean climate.

## PLATERESCO
An early Renaissance style ushered in by "Catholic Kings" Ferdinand and Isabella. Its ornate lacelike carvings and ironwork closely resemble silverwork.

## PLAZA MAJOR
The main square, lined with a covered arcade; found in almost every village, town, and city of Spain, it serves as a community forum.

## PORRON
Wine carafe with a long pointed spout from which to drink directly without touching the lips.

## REJAS
Iron grilles that pierce the stucco of a house's exterior and cover the window openings.

## VARGEUNO
Typical Spanish cabinet, which was placed on an elaborate stand or built with four carved legs.

# FESTIVALS AND TRADITIONS

### DIA DE LOS REYES MAGOS
The Day of the Magi. Celebrated throughout Spain on the 12th day after Christmas. For children in Spain, it is not Santa Claus who bears gifts, but rather the Three Kings who brought presents to the Baby Jesus. On this night a *"roscón"* cake is eaten, and whoever discovers the coin hidden in the cake is declared king or queen for the evening.

### EL ROCIO
A pilgrimage to the church of the Virgin in the tiny town of Rocio in the province of Huelva. For 10 days beginning April 19th, gypsies from all over Huelva and Seville dress in Andalusian costumes and ride on horses or carts decorated with flowers.

### FERIA DE ABRIL
The April Fair. Annual fair in Seville from the 18th to the 23rd. What began as a livestock fair in the 19th century is now a fiesta of wine, bulls, horses, and flamenco.

### LAS FALLAS
In the city of Valencia, a feast that dates from the Middle Ages in honor of Saint Joseph. On the night of March 19, *rallas,* or fantastically big wood-and-wax statues, are burned to conclude a week of fireworks, bullfights, and religious processions.

### NOCHE VIEJA
New Year's Eve. All over Spain and particularly in Madrid's Puerta del Sol, people gather and try to eat and swallow twelve grapes while the clock strikes twelve. Those who succeed are said to have good luck in the new year.

### ROMERIA
All over Spain and at different times of the year, a pilgrimage by a large procession or crowd to an isolated church or hermitage, often dedicated to the Virgin Mary. Local girls are often named after the chapels: Rocio, Pilar (patron of Zaragoza), Monserrat, or Guadalupe.

## SAN FERMIN
Festival that occurs in Pamplona during the first or second week of July and includes the running of the bulls through the streets on their way to the bullfight.

## SAN ISIDRO
May 15th. Two weeks of festivities follow in honor of the patron saint of Madrid.

## SAN JUAN
Celebrated all over Spain on the 24th of June in honor of Saint John. On the night of the 23rd of June, a giant bonfire is lit on the mountain of Montjuic in Barcelona, preceded by a week of firecrackers and fireworks.

## SEMANA SANTA
Holy Week, or the week before Easter. Celebrated all over Spain, with fervent processions that feature elaborate, *pasos,* or floats, with groups of life-size statues. The most spectacular is in Seville, where the participants are dressed as penitents. In Catalonia, villagers act out the Passion of Christ.

## SIESTA
The afternoon break, from one or two until four or five P.M. Most common in Andalusia, where the extreme heat almost makes it necessary to close down in the middle of the day.

## TERTULIA
An informal club hour after work. People gather in bars over a glass of wine and tapas to discuss anything from literature to politics.

# FOOD AND DRINK

### CAFE CON LECHE
Coffee with milk, usually served at breakfast.

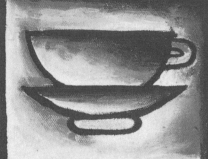

### CAFE CORTADO
A small cup of espresso served with a drop or two of milk.

### CAFE SOLO
Black coffee, usually served at night.

### CHORIZO
A spicy Spanish sausage, redolent of garlic.

### FABADA
A thick soup of beans and sausage, typical of Asturias.

### CHURROS
Pieces of deep-fried dough sprinkled with sugar, usually served with mugs of thick, rich hot chocolate.

### GAZPACHO
A cold soup from Andalusia, made of tomato, cucumber, green pepper, and onion and seasoned with garlic. It is often thickened with fresh bread crumbs.

### HORCHATA
A cold and refreshing drink popular in the summer. It is made from the chufa, or earth almond, a root that grows near Valencia.

### JAMON
Ham. Cured for up to two years, *jamón ibérico* is highly prized for its distinctive sweet flavor. *Jamón serrano,* named for the dry Spanish sierras, is cured for one year and is less moist than the *ibérico*.

## JEREZ
Sherry. A fortified wine from Jerez de la Frontera; produced by English emigrants to Spain in the 17th century.

## MANTECADOS
Small almond cakes, found in almost every bakery.

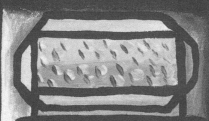

## PAELLA VALENCIANA
A rich dish typical of Valencia and probably invented in the region south of the city where rice is cultivated. Paella is cooked in a special pan about the size of a tire and includes a variety of meats and seafoods. Saffron gives it its traditional yellow color.

## SANGRIA
An iced punch consisting of wine, fruit juice, lemonade, soda, brandy, and slices of orange and lemon. Typical of Andalusia but consumed all over Spain.

## OLIVAS; ACEITE DE OLIVA
The olive is one of Spain's basic crops, and olive oil is a fundamental ingredient of Spanish cooking. Olive trees dot the countryside along the coast of southeastern Spain and throughout Andalusia.

## TAPAS
Appetizers or "grazing" food. Throughout the day, or before meals, people congregate in corner bars and snack on sardines, cheese, chorizo, *calamares* (squid), and *jamón* (ham). Tapas are often accompanied by a glass of wine or beer.

## MANCHEGO
Cheese from the Castile region, a basic offering at a tapas bar.

## TORTILLA

An omelette made with either potatoes, spinach, onions, or a combination of the three.

## TURRON

A Spanish version of torrone. A special dessert made primarily of honey and almonds and eaten only around Christmas-time. *Turrón* from Jijona is hard and includes whole almonds wrapped in nougat. *Turrón* from Alicante is a softer, crumbly version in which the almonds are pulverized.

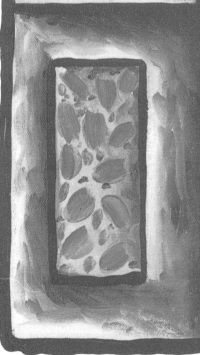

# MUSIC AND DANCE

## CASTANUELAS

In English, castanets. Composed of two pieces of hardwood and suspended from the fingers with a string, the instrument is most commonly used by flamenco dancers to create a rhythmic snapping, sound.

## FLAMENCO

A gypsy or folk tradition of song and dance, now often performed in *tablaos,* or nightclubs. The song expresses a range of emotion from exultation to despair. The dance interprets the emotions in movement.

## GAITAS

Bagpipes played in Galicia, where Celtic traditions abound and where the landscape is reminiscent of Ireland.

## GUITARRA

The guitar is particularly associated with Spain, where it dates back to the 12th century. By the 18th century, it had become the most popular instrument to accompany flamenco.

## SARDANA

Folkdance from the Catalonia region. Circles of 10 to 12 people dance around holding their hands together and up in the air. Dancers wear the requisite rope-soled shoes known as espadrilles.

## SEVILLANA

Expressive dance, known by that name at least since the mid-19th century, performed especially in Seville during the *Feria de Abril,* as well as at weddings and even to celebrate local football victories.

# Costume

### BOINA
The beret, original to the Basque country, which includes four provinces (one of which is in France).

### BOLERO
A short, sleeveless jacket, usually worn by peasants.

### CABEZUDO
One of the large cardboard heads worn in festivals and processions.

### ESPADRILLES
Soft cloth shoes with rope soles, worn for the Sardana dance typical of Catalonia.

### MAJA
A term for the lower- and middle-class men and women of the 18th century, who affected a style of dress depicted in Goya's prints and drawings. The men wore black broad-rimmed hats; the women wore black mantillas.

### MANTILLA
A large scarf, often made of lace and supported with a *peinta* or comb, worn by Spanish women since the beginning of the 18th century.

### PEINTA
The comb, usually made of tortoise shell, used to hold the mantilla up and away from the face.

### PUNTILLA
A typically Spanish lace, made by hand with wooden bat-shaped bobbins, or *bolillos*.

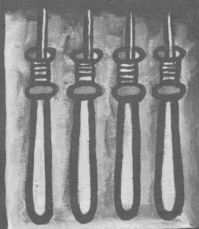

### TAPALO
An overlarge shawl, usually made of wool chambray edged in a deep silk fringe.

### TRAJE DE LUCES
The matador's costume (translated as "suit of lights"). The skullcap worn with it has stylized bull's horns, and the top is decorated with a stylized bull's-eye motif.

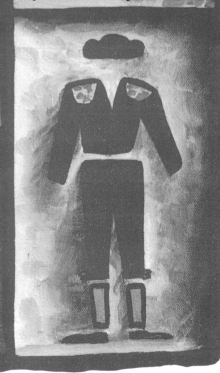

## A

Aalto, Alvar, 212
Agua de Limon, Alayor, 230–37
Agudo Clará, Ignacio, 70, 72
Alcazar, Segovia, 6, 100
  glazed tiles of, 28
  Patio de las Muñecas, 41
Alfabia, Mallorca, 60–69
Alfonso XII, King, 113
Alfonso XIII, King, furniture from the period of, 160
Amat, Fernando, 75–82
Antiguo Hospital de la Concepción, 128
Arab influence, 89, 96, 119
Archivo de Indias, Seville, 28
*artesonadas* (coffered ceilings), 118
Art Nouveau style, 153
Aubusson carpet, 153, 157
*azulejos* (glazed tiles), 28, 42, 45, 90, 118
Azulete, 23

## B

Baccarat crystal, 114, 115
Balearic Islands:
  carpets from the, 140
  furniture of the, 234
  paintings from the, 178
Baroque style, 28, 30, 60, 61, 86, 92, 126, 142
Barrio de Santa Cruz, Seville, 172
Bassó, Carles, 48
Blanes, Miguel Servera, 266
boathouses, 264–65
Bonetti, Mattia, 77
bullfight (*corrida de toros*), 10, 13, 27

## C

Café Costes chairs, 207
cafés, 24, 26, 27

*California Roll* (sculpture), 198
Campbell home, Seville, 172–75
Campanet, Palma de Mallorca, 266–73
Can Llatxe (Saint Lazarus), Ibiza, 259–63
Carrelet, Catherine, 279
Carrelet home, Ibiza, 279–84
Casa Battló, Barcelona, 186
Casa Gremial Dels Velers o de la Seda, Barcelona, 100
Casa Lleo i Morera, 48
Casa Milá, Barcelona, 75, 153–58
Casas, Ramon, 102
Casa Thomas, Barcelona, 46
Casa Viçens, Barcelona, 95–99
Catálogo, 289–97
Catany, Toni, 218
  apartment of, 218–23
Cathedral of Seville, Gothic, 28
ceilings, coffered, 118
chapels, 91, 92, 104
Charles IV furniture, 112, 113
Chaves Mendoza family, 128
Chillida, Eduardo, 245
Chippendale Revival furniture, 177
Christian architecture, 28
Clusella, Amadeu, 204
Coelho, Duarte Pinto, 52, 54, 128, 130, 133
Cohen, Elaine Lustig, 248, 250, 251
Cohen home, Mallorca, 248–51
*Corberebus* (sculpture), 199
Corbero, Xavier, 196, 198, 199
Corbero house, Esplugas, 196–203
*corrida de toros* (bullfight), 10, 13, 27
Cortijo San Andres, 14
Cortines, Enrique, 166
Cortines, José, 166

Cortines, Loupe, 166
Costa i Llobera, Miguel, 180, 181, 184
Costa i Llobera house, Pollensa, 180–85
courtyards, 41, 75, 105, 175
Cusachs, José, 102

## D

De Cardenas, Felix, 273
Delaunay, Sonia, 250
del Montseny, Count and Countess, 153
De Natura (store), 238
Deroulede, Sabine, 238
Doménech i Montaner, Luis, 16, 46, 48, 186
doorways, 37
Dos i Una, 188
Duchamp, Marcel, 80
Dufour, Joseph, 154
Dupin, Fanny, 259
Dupin, Patrick, 259

## E

Engles, Betty, 172, 173, 174
Engles, Campbell, 172, 173, 174
English style, 157, 176–79, 230, 232

## F

Fabregas de Sentmenat, Eulalia, 144, 145, 146
  residence in Esplugas, 144–52
Fabregas de Santmenat, Ramon, 144
family homes, 136–85
Fernandino architecture, 125
Fernandino furniture, 123, 183
Ferdinand VII, furniture from the period of, 156
Ferran, Vicenç, 188, 192

apartment of, 188–95
Font i Carreras, August, 10
Fontsere i Mestres, Josep, 23
Fundacio Pilar i Joan Miró, 266

## G

Garcia, Torres, 102
Gardner, Ava, ix, 84
Garouste, Elizabeth, 77
Gaudí i Cornet, Antonio, 30, 45, 50, 75, 78, 79, 95, 98, 153, 186, 209
*Gavina* (sculpture), 199
Georgian-style furniture, 177, 178
Gil de la Calleja, José Luis, 230
Godia, Francisco, 102, 107
Godia, Inés, 102
Gothic influence, 32, 268
Gris, Juan, 102
Guinovart, Josep, 269
Gutierrez Solona, José, 102

## H

Hacienda de Bugalmoro, near Seville, 86–94
Hacienda Micones, near Seville, 166–71
Hilario, Federico, 274
  vacation home of, 274–78
Homar, Gaspar, 48

## I

Ibara, Juan, 86
images of Spain, 4–15
Ingenio, El, 21
Isabelino style, 125, 139, 140, 150, 184
Isabelino Rococo Revival furniture, 153

**J**

Josefa, Maria, 274
  vacation home of, 274–78
Jover family, 95
Jover de Herrero, Fabiola, 95
Jujol, Josep Maria, 209

**L**

Leone, Eduardo, 118
living in Spain, 16–27
Llimos, Robert, 269
Llobera family mansion,
  Pollensa, 159–65
Llopis, Francesca, 77
Louis XV-style furniture, 262
Louis XVI-inspired furniture,
  146
Loyola, Saint Ignatius, 110

**M**

Mahón, Minorca, 176
majolica plates, 142
Mallorcan style, 159, 183
Manas, Juan Antonio, 188, 192
  apartment of, 188–95
Mariscal, Javier, 77, 211, 264
Masso, Agnes, 252
Masso, Alejandro, 252
Masso home, Pedraza,
  252–58
Maurer, Ingo, 79, 80, 207,
  212
Meritos, Marquise de, 118
Micon, Tomás, Marquis de
  Meritos, 166
Mila y Camps, Pablo, 153
Minacelli family, 86, 89
*mirador* (overhanging
  balcony), 38, 86
Miró, Joan, 84
*modernismo,* Catalan, 28, 46,
  50, 75, 95, 186, 209
Modern style, 186–227
Moorish influence, 28, 30, 41,
  92, 95, 97, 118, 126, 173,
  281

Moron, Lluís, 204
Moron loft, Barcelona,
  204–208
Moxo family, 110
Mudejar style, 28, 50, 118,
  119
Muñoz, Lucio, 245
Muñoz, Paco, 238, 240, 245
Muñoz home, Pedraza,
  238–47

**N**

Neoclassical style, 28, 42, 58,
  121, 144, 154, 221
Noguchi, Isamu, 77, 211

**P**

palaces, 100–135
Palacio Bardaji, Ibiza, 70
Palacio de la Condesa de
  Lebrija, Seville, 118–27
Palacio de los Chaves
  Mendoza, Trujillo, 128–35
Palacio de los Montero, Ibiza,
  138–43
Palacio Moxo, Barcelona,
  110–17
Parellada, Ines, 209
Parellada, Ramon, 209, 211
Parellada apartment,
  Barcelona, 209–13
Parc Güell, Barcelona, 45
Parque de la Ciutadella,
  Barcelona, 23
Pascual, Don Mariano, 26
patios, 172, 173, 175
Patronato Municipal de
  Turismo de Barcelona, 48
Pastor, Pura Orti, 70, 72
Pedralbes, monastery of,
  guest house of, 102
Pedrera, La, Barcelona, 75,
  77
Philip V, King, 10, 134
Picasso, Pablo, IX, 102
Pilma (store), 224

Pinohermosa Palace, Madrid,
  52
Planells, Angel, 77
Plaza de Toros:
  Barcelona, 10
  Seville, 10
Poveda Amadon, Aurora, 230
Puente del Arzobispo, 133
Puig, Blai, 224
  apartment of, 224–27

**R**

Renaissance influence, 28
Riart, Carlos, 77, 79
Riera, Mireia, 48
Rimbaud, Arthur, 250
Riquer, Carlos, 138
Rococo Revival furniture, 150
Rococo style, 64, 66, 126,
  220, 281
Roman antiquities, 118, 119,
  166

**S**

Sagrada Familia cathedral,
  Barcelona, 30
Sanchez Barbudo, Carmen,
  14
Sanchez Barbudo, Salvador,
  14
San Gervasio, Barcelona, 188
San Mori, Marquise de, 110,
  115
Santa & Cole, 213
Savonnerie carpet, 146
Serrat, Juan Manuel, 201
shops, 18, 21
Sorolla, Joaquín, 139
Starck, Phillippe, 207
style, elements of Spanish,
  28–49
Subirachs, Josep Maria, 103
Szenczi, Brigitte, 188, 192, 193
  apartment of, 188–95

**T**

Taberna del Alcalde, La,
  Pedraza, 26
Tápies, Antoni, 245
Tiffon, Maria Luisa, 196
Tito (artist), 214–17
Torres Gassana, F., 97
*traje de luces,* 13
Tusquets, Oscar, 23

**U**

Umbracle, Barcelona, 23

**V**

vacation homes, 228–88
Velázquez, Diego, 156
Viaplana, Vicenc, 204, 207
Viçens, Manuel, 95
Vinçón, Barcelona, 75
Vives Campomar, Antonia,
  176
Vives Campomar house,
  Mahón, 176–78

**W**

Wagner, Richard, 72
wall decoration, 32, 35
Williams, Harris H., 83, 84
windmill, 285
women, images of Spanish, 8

**Y**

Ya Ya Ho lamp, 207

**Z**

Zuloaga, Ignacio, 139

# STYLE LIBRARY

An ongoing series of high-quality all-color publications that focus on international areas of cultural and domestic interest.

## French Style

Suzanne Slesin and Stafford Cliff/ Photographs by Jacques Dirand

*"Not only an important contribution to the literature of interior decorating, but also a touchstone for our times."* – Los Angeles Herald Examiner

For centuries the French have been celebrated for their *art de vivre*, and *French Style* is a book that captures the charm, vitality, and elegance of the contemporary French life-style as it is reflected in that country's interiors. Town and country houses, flats, lofts, ateliers, and chateaux demonstrate the range of French design tastes and provide many translatable decorating ideas. *French Style* exudes that special quality, a rare blend of magic, elegance, and sophistication for which the French are famous.

The directory provides a listing of sources for French and French-style antiques and contemporary furnishings.

## JAPANESE STYLE

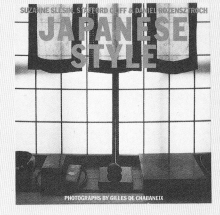

Suzanne Slesin, Stafford Cliff, and Daniel Rozensztroch/Photographs by Gilles de Chabaneix

*"A mesmerizing look at the rarefied and rarely visited Japanese homes."* – Vogue

A stylish, sophisticated, and often unexpected look at how the Japanese live today, as expressed through interior design, *Japanese Style* captures the richness and diversity of modern Japan. In almost 800 full-color photographs, the book presents a wide range of houses and apartments – from architect-designed contemporary homes to centuries-old farmhouses and inns. The locations include a fashion designer's luxurious Tokyo duplex, a stunning house and garden on a hillside near Kyoto, a traditional geisha house, and the country house of the renowned potter Shoji Hamada.

*Japanese Style* holds many lessons – and delights – for Westerners as it evokes the never-ending romance of Japan.

## English Style

Suzanne Slesin and Stafford Cliff/ Photographs by Ken Kirkwood

*"A singularly beautiful and evocative look at the mix of formality, coziness, and comfort that is complex yet instantly recognizable as English Style."* – Chicago Tribune

*English Style* richly illustrates the value of tradition and ingenuity in today's English interior design. From a grand manor house replete with chintzes to a London factory loft furnished with graphic severity, from a gabled country cottage to a Victorian terrace house with original William Morris wallpaper, each of these splended interiors is quintessentially English.

More than 600 glorious full-color photographs accompany an informative text, and a catalogue of sources of English furnishings is included as well.

## Greek Style

Suzanne Slesin, Stafford Cliff, and Daniel Rozensztroch/Photographs by Gilles de Chabaneix

*"The photographs...are seductive... what the simple rural style should be."* – New York Times

Rustic and elegant, ancient and modern, minimal and yet rich in detail, the style of Greece is one of exciting contrasts. *Greek Style* captures not only the authentic simplicity of Greek interior design, but also the remarkable liveliness of Greek culture. Here you will discover the dramatic geographical range of Greece, from the northern mainland, with its mountains and Oriental influences, to the Cyclades, Ionian, and Dodecanese islands, with their whitewashed villages clinging to rocky hills. Centuries-old family estates, the turquoise and pink studio of a local artist, and the cliff-top and beach-front dwellings of newcomers – all celebrate an unforgettable and enduring stylistic tradition.

## CARIBBEAN STYLE

Suzanne Slesin, Stafford Cliff, Jack Berthelot, Martine Gaumé, and Daniel Rozensztroch/ Photographs by Gilles de Chabaneix

*"A handsome book...that presents the Caribbean islands as a rich and distinctive aesthetic experience."* – New York Times Book Review

A unique blend of travel book and design book, *Caribbean Style* offers a previously unseen view of the architecture, interior design, gardens, and life-style of Guadeloupe, Martinique, St. Barthélemy, Antigua, Nevins, Montserrat, Barbados, Haiti, and Jamaica. The book includes chapters on plantation houses, town houses, popular houses, contemporary houses, gardens, island vegetation and colors, climate and crops, and cultural heritage.

## INDIAN STYLE

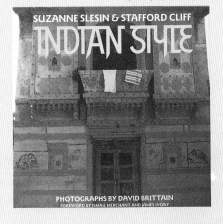

Suzanne Slesin and Stafford Cliff/ Photographs by David Brittain

India. Maharajas' palaces. Family homes from the era of the great trading routes. Houseboats moored on peaceful lakes. Stone farmhouses in the foothills of the Himalayas. Perhaps no other place in the world has such a vital and unexpected design tradition as the Indian subcontinent. *Indian Style* meticulously observes and brings vividly to life this vast, eclectic culture. With more than 700 full-color photographs, this exciting collage of colors, textures, flavors, seasons, and panoramas chronicles an exotic past while revealing the richly varied present of this mysterious and majestic country.